The Possessed Individual
technology and postmodernity

CultureTexts

Arthur and Marilouise Kroker   *General Editors*

CultureTexts is a series of creative explorations in theory, politics and culture at the fin de millennium. Thematically focussed around key theoretical debates in the postmodern condition, the CultureTexts series challenges received discourses in art, social and political theory, feminism, psychoanalysis, value inquiry, science and technology, the body, and critical aesthetics. Taken individually, contributions to CultureTexts represent the forward breaking-edge of postmodern theory and practice.

Titles

THE POSSESSED INDIVIDUAL
technology and postmodernity

Arthur Kroker

MACMILLAN

First published 1992

Published by
MACMILLAN PRESS LTD
Houndmills, Basingstoke, Hampshire, RG21 2XS
and London
Companies and representatives throughout the world

ISBN 0-333-57550-4

A catalogue record for this book is available from the British Library.

Printed in Canada.

Acknowledgements

I wish to thank Marilouise Kroker, Michael Weinstein and David Cook for their insightful intellectual reading of the manuscript in preparation. I am also grateful to Alexis Gosselin for her invaluable assistance as well as to my friends, William Leiss and Marilyn Lawrence, for the meditative space of their virtual cottage. Research for this book was facilitated by a grant from the *Social Sciences and Humanities Research Council of Canada*.

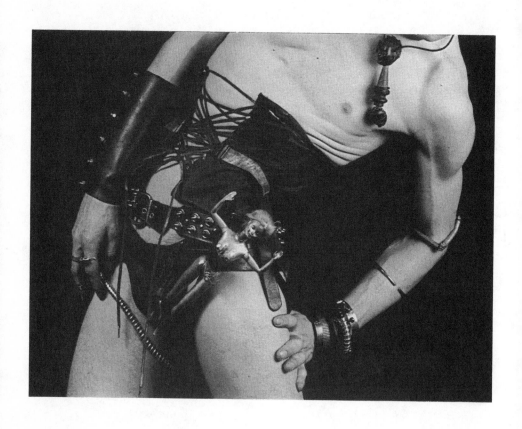

Photograph: Linda Dawn Hammond
Martial (Three Part BodySeries)

CONTENTS

Preface

VIRTUAL REALITY
IS WHAT THE POSSESSED INDIVIDUAL IS
POSSESSED BY

The Possessed Individual rubs America against contemporary French thought. What results is a dramatic reinterpretation of French theory as a prophetic analysis of the speed-life of the twenty-first century, and a critical rethinking of the politics and culture of the technological dynamo. This book is a hinge between the mirror of seduction that is America today and the philosophical ruptures of French thought, from Sartre and Camus to Baudrillard and Virilio. And why the fascination with French thought? Because its discourse is a theoretical foreground to America's political background: fractal thinkers in whose central images one finds the key power configurations of the American hologram. Read the French, therefore, to learn a language for thinking anew the empire of technology.

Contemporary French thought consists of a creative, dynamic and highly original account of technological society. Refusing the pragmatic account of technology as freedom and eschewing a tragic description of technology as degeneration, an arc of twentieth-century French thinkers, from Jean Baudrillard and Roland Barthes to Paul Virilio, Jean-François Lyotard, Deleuze and Guattari and Foucault have presented a description of technology as cynical power. Indeed, what might be called the key impulse of French "bimodernism" has been to explore the mutation of technology within a series of critical discourses: technology as pure speed (Virilio), technology as simulation (Baudrillard), the rhetoric of technology (Barthes), technology as a desiring-machine (Deleuze and Guattari), technology as aesthetics (Lyotard) and technologies of subjectivity (Foucault). Here, technological society is described under the sign of possessed individualism: an invasive power where life is enfolded within the dynamic technological language of virtual reality. Virtual reality? That is the recoding of human experience by the algorithmic codes of computer wetware. No longer alienation, reification or simulation as stages in the technological dialectic of social emancipation and human domination, but virtuality now as the dominant sign of contemporary technological society. Indeed, virtual reality—the world of digital dreams come alive—is what the possessed individual is possessed by.

What emerges from the French mind, then, is an account of technological society that can be immediately and massively influential because it is a mirror of technology in the postmodern scene. This means that the reception of French thought in the outmoded form of post-structuralism has always been a trompe l'oeil deflecting attention from the key contribution of French thinkers as theorists of technology par excellence; that is, as brilliant interpreters of the virtual phase of technological society. Thus, for example, while American thought is trapped in a pragmatic description of technology as liberation, the French discourse on technology begins with the violent exteriorization of the self, actually producing an eerie and disturbing account of cynical technology. Of technology, that is, in its fully aestheticized phase where speaking means the rhetoric machine, where living means simulation, where the self *is* a desiring-machine, and where feeling is a rhizomatic network. To enter into the French mind—into Deleuze and Guattari's decoded flows of the doubled sign, into Virilio's world of speed-power, into Barthes's melancholy domain of "anachronic subjectivity"—is really to enter into the deepest recesses of postmodern subjectivity. The reversible nature of their articulations means that to read the French is finally to understand the theoretical mechanisms by which power functions in America. And even more. To become entangled in the internal debates which storm across French thought—Baudrillard's break with Foucault, Camus's refusal of Sartre, the implacable opposition between Lyotard and Barthes—is to become entwined in the deepest cultural debates of the *fin de millennium*. To think technology, that is, against the grain of justice, and to meditate again with Camus the question of the coeval nature of reason and murder as the ruling ethos of technological society. Just as Camus once murmured that "to begin to think is to be undermined," to reflect upon the doubled sign of French thought is finally to undermine not only the technological society outside but, more disturbingly, one's own subjectivity. French thought, therefore, as a violent decoding and recoding of the American way, which is to say, of all the world, since America is today the global hologram.

1

POSSESSED INDIVIDUALISM: TECHNOLOGY AND THE FRENCH POSTMODERN

Possessed Individualism

Man Ray's *Fashion Photo* is a perfect visual description of possessed individualism. Here, the world is in its terminal phase of aestheticization: lips without a speaking subject and the body in dreams under the dark but charming sky of all the signs of seduction. There are no voices, no memories, only the aestheticized signs of the portrait of clouds and the image of the reclining body as indications of the purely cynical nature of the trompe l'oeil. The signs of difference are themselves indifferent. A topology of driftworks and subjectivity in the reverie of ruins remains. No

Man Ray, *Fashion Photograph* © VISART

longer "possessive individualism" under the Lockean sign of private property and use value, but now possessed individualism under the sign of abuse value. The aestheticization of experience to such a point of excess that nature, subjectivity, and desire migrate into seduction: into a game of chance and indifferent relations of pure positionality.

"Possessed individualism" is subjectivity to a point of aesthetic excess that the self no longer has any real existence, only a perspectival appearance as a site where all the referents converge and implode. Subjectivity, therefore, which is created qut of the ruins of abuse value, a designer self which emerges from the cancellation of all the signs. An *apparent* self whose memories can be fantastic reveries of a past which never really existed, because it occupies a purely virtual space—the space of an accidental topology and seductive contiguity of aesthetic effects. No longer a private subject in a public space, but a public self in a private imaginary time: a parallel self among many others drifting aimlessly, but no less violently for that, in parallel worlds. And so, Man Ray was prophetic. *Fashion Photo* is constructed purely as an aesthetic trompe l'oeil, with its edges marked by two simu-visions: one photographic (the reclining woman) and the other a product of a painterly gesture (the portrait on the wall). Here, there are no human presences, only "significant images" that trace the implosion of subjectivity into a charmless universe of seduction, and of the body into a disappearing trace of an imposed imaginary.

At one time, it was still possible to speak of the postmodern subject as a possessive individual, that is, as an originary possessor or calculative owner of acquisitive and appropriative values. This would be the contractual self of early political economy where the subject represented the terminus ad quem of property rights so privileged in primitive capitalism. The possessive individual, then, as an energizing agent which, driven on by the inequality of property rights, was eager to lay waste to the order of the production machine. Now, however, it is the reverse. Not the possessive individual as the consumer par excellence, but the possessed individual as itself an object of consumption. No longer the production machine of primitive capitalism driven onwards by use value, but now the consumption machine of designer capitalism, the point where the subject is itself actually consumed by the laws of abuse value, seduced and disciplined in an indifferent game of chance and probability. And not an ideologically constituted self either, but a rhetorical subject, that is, possessed individualism as the exhausted sign of the disappearance of ideology into the language of rhetoric as the war machine. Horizoned by forgetfulness, charmed by seduction, disciplined by the codes of cynical power, the possessed individual is the form taken by nihilism in the last dying days of rationalism. Nietzsche's "maggot man."

The Judge-Penitent

I discovered that while waiting for the masters with their rods, we should, like Copernicus, reverse the reasoning to win out. Inasmuch as one couldn't condemn others without immediately judging oneself, one had to overwhelm oneself to have the right to judge others. Inasmuch as every judge some day ends up as a penitent, one had to travel the road in the opposite direction and practice the profession of penitent to be able to end up as a judge.

Albert Camus, *The Fall*

But then the French mind has always exhibited a fascination for the study of subjectivity as the ruins within, comprising on the whole a brilliant meditation on the dark, and fatally charming, universe of the possessed individual. Think, for example, of Sartre and Camus who, if they can summarize so eloquently in their thought the fate of the modernist subject in political history, also represent a clear and present division between the final disappearance of the possessive individual of the age of classical liberalism and the triumphant emergence of the possessed individual as the inheritor of the nihilist legacy. Indeed, it is the ultimate failure of Sartre and Camus to think beyond the horizon of the modernist project which represents the beginning-point for contemporary French theory. French intellectuality of the late twentieth-century represents nothing less than shock waves spreading out from the failure of that fateful double sign of the French mind— Sartre and Camus—to resolve a problem which they posed with their lives, but were unable, in the end, to solve.

To speak of Sartre and Camus, France's two principal modernist thinkers of the mid-twentieth century, is really to awaken to an older debate in the western mind between the nihilist (like Camus), who is finally reduced to the role of a witness testifying to the presence of evil, like a biblical prophet who has drunk so deeply of the banal darkness of everyday life that he can only mutter imprecations, and the political activist (like Sartre) who chooses immersion in history rather than silence, and for whom ambivalence over the question of the nature of good and evil, of love and murder, is suppressed in favor of political commitment. A political engagement to a certain vision of history which, if it loses its shadow of ambivalence and paradox, also acquires the strength of clarity and comprehensiveness.

To meditate, then, on Camus and Sartre is really to speak of an older quarrel between Nietzsche and Marx, of two deeply contrasting, and equally critical, visions of politics and life: of Nietzsche's tragic pronouncements on the will to power and Marx's decision to choose history and with it the will to power rather than sacrifice justice. Nietzsche and Marx, then, as a deeper debate between individual freedom and collective justice, of what it means to live today at that point where personal autobiography crosses over into public history. Camus, therefore, as the ambivalent individualist who might begin in *The Rebel* with a choice between metaphysical rebellion (revolt against God) and historical rebellion (political revolt) and who might write in *The Myth of Sisyphus* about suicide and absurd experience; but who ends up in that great Nietzschean book, *The Fall*, by choosing for himself the role of the judge-penitent. Jean-Paul Sartre, then, as the avenging judge of contemporary political history; and Camus as its judge-penitent. Thus speaks the Camus of *The Fall*:

> In solitude and fatigue, one is after all inclined to take oneself for a prophet. When all is said and done, that's really what I am, having taken refuge in a desert of stones, fogs, and stagnant waters—an empty prophet for shabby times. Elijah without a messiah, choked with fever and alcohol, my back against this moldy door, my finger raised toward a threatening sky, showering imprecations on lawless men who cannot endure any judgement. For they can't endure it, très cher, and that's the whole question. He who clings to law that does not fear the judgment that reinstates him in an order that he believes in. But the keenest of human torments is to be judged without a law. Yet we are in that torment. Deprived of their natural curb, the judges, loosed at random, are racing through their job. Hence we have to try to go faster than they, don't we? And it's a real madhouse. Prophets and quacks multiply; they hasten to get there with a good law or a flawless organization before the world is deserted. Fortunately, I arrived! I am the end and the beginning; I announce the law. In short, I am the judge-penitent.[1]

Camus died early and romantically, a poet-philosopher in a car accident with a copy of Nietzsche's *The Gay Science* on the seat beside him. More than most, his thought focussed upon and defined the central tension of contemporary politics: our living in a nowhere time between the death of God and the death of History, with an inability to be either a Christian judge (a moralist) or a political judge (the Commissar). Camus's life was lived within and against all totalities: he could be neither a Christian nor a Communist, but was that rarest of thinkers: a radical individualist who travelled deeply within himself on an internal migration into the interstices of the possessed individual, as thought itself lived out its fate at the meridian.

What is thought at the meridian? It is the life of authentic thought which exists in rebellion against absolutes: against religious absolutes (the death of God) and against historical absolutes (the death of ideology).

Between religion and history, between nihilism and history: that is, thought which, for Camus, is at the meridian because it is that irreconcilable point of division between an "absolute freedom which mocks at justice" and an "absolute justice which denies freedom".[2] So then, Camus, the thinker whose intellectuality was forged on the anvil of two great world events: the refusal of God with the cold dawn of secular rationalism in the West; and the refusal of history with the triumph of state fascism in Germany and state Communism in the East. A political philosopher without a country except that of the deterritorialized terrain of the intellectual imagination. But then, as an Algerian, he was always a Mediterranean thinker, a philosopher whose ideas germinated under the blinding sun of the sea and desert.

Camus again:

> The profound conflict of this century is perhaps not so much between the German ideologies of history and Christian political concepts, which in a certain way are accomplices, as between German dreams and Mediterranean traditions, between the violence of adolescence and virile strength, between nostalgia, rendered more acute by knowledge and by books, and courage reinforced and enlightened by the experience of life—in other words, between history and nature. But German ideology, in this sense, has come into an inheritance. It consummates twenty centuries of abortive struggle against nature in the name of a historic god and then of a deified history.[3]

If, against Sartre's final declamation that "man is a useless passion," Camus could finally say "I revolt, therefore *we* exist," it is because he was finally a thinker of the solar night, a Mediterranean within whose imagination "civilization faces two ways awaiting its dawn," mindful, that is, of the irreconcilable conflict in the European mind between historical absolutism and the demand for freedom which finds its purchase in intelligence which is "intimately related to the blinding light of the sun."[4]

So too, for Sartre. All of his intellectual life, which is to say *all* of his life for in his autobiography, *The Words*, Sartre speaks of his vocation as a thinker, beginning with his childhood when he first realized that he would write so as not to die, Sartre struggles to mediate the modern dialectic. It went by different terms. In the *Critique of Dialectical Reason*, it is the struggle between falling into the mud of everyday existence, the practico-inert, and the struggle to transcend the historical particularities

of domination. In *Being and Nothingness*, it was the dialectical confrontation between being for-itself and in-itself. Later, it would be defined as
the struggle between "seriality" (where we become technical automatons,
stamped individuals) and "fused groups"—collective solidarities organized around a political project, united by emotions of solidarity and
struggle, and waiting to strike.[5] For Sartre, to struggle publicly for justice,
to abandon the absurdist impulse of romantic individualism on behalf
of collective justice, is to give meaning to history. It is to overcome
seriality, the mud of the practico-inert, to transcend, overcome and
practically renew political history by collective struggle.

And so, the radically practical question arises: What are the limits of
domination today? At one time, we could speak comfortably of the
struggle for freedom as a loosening of unwanted bonds of political
coercion by a deliberate transgression of The Rules—a revolt against
arbitrary power. But in postmodern society, the society anticipated by
Camus's judge-penitent, rules exist only as a seductive challenge to
transgress them. Today, can we ever be certain that the order of
domination exists as a comfortable assurance of limits placed on our
freedom, and that as Michel Foucault, perhaps meditating on the judge-
penitent, says: "Power as a pure limit set on freedom is, at least in our
society, the general form of its acceptability"?[6] Without the promise of
power as a limiting condition, the order of freedom would lose its
moment of seduction and we would finally be able to say publicly what
had heretofore only been thought unconsciously: that now only judgement, not freedom, is desirable. What we desire is the abolition of
freedom, the placing of limits by judgment on the limitlessness of
experience: on all of the big signifiers— God, money, sex, class, and the
unconscious. Maybe the secret of power today is precisely the seduction
of domination that it contains and always promises to secrete: the
promise of limits under the sign of judgement to save us from limitlessness, from an order of existence with no rules, no laws, only excess, only
challenge. Not so much, therefore, the challenge of freedom, but the
seduction of the labyrinth of domination, the real seduction of cynical
power, as the primal of the postmodern mind.

Or perhaps it is the opposite. Not the order of law as a sinecure against
judgments without law, but the challenge of excess as a way of
overcoming the limits of judgments within the law. Perhaps the last

temptation of Camus was to become a practitioner of abuse value, the penitent on the road to judgment who reverses the meaning of the order of reason. Not judgments within the law as a way of reconciling justice and freedom, but judging against the law, beyond the law, as excessive points of challenge to the complicity of murder and justice, as a way of overcoming the limits of unreason. Camus, then, as the first and best of all the possessed individuals, the thinker who made of his own intellectuality and of his deepest subjectivity an experimental zone for abuse value, for introducing a great and unsettling reversibility into the dialectic of reason. And Sartre too. For if Sartre could begin with a political project under the sign of possessive individualism—the radical critique of the three European terrorisms, state capitalism, state social-ism, and state fascism—then he also ended with the dark knowledge that the order of domination had mutated into a different, and more alarming, order of events. That may be why the militant Sartre of *The Words* and the *Critique of Dialectical Reason* culminates in his thought in the Old Testament prophet of *Nausea* and his searing essay on Czechoslovakia, muttering dark imprecations against our current posses-sion now by the demonic force of "The Thing".[7] At the end of their lives, then, the intellectual trajectories of Sartre and Camus crossed over one another, and cancelled the other out. Camus may have begun with a refusal of the dialectic of reason and its accompanying revolts against God and against history, but he ultimately became a Sartrean moralist. He may have begun with the entanglement of the absurd and the question of suicide, but his thought culminated with a recovery of dialectics: with a political tension between the realm of the practico-inert and solar thought. And Sartre may have initiated his thought as a political rebellion against the impassivity and paradoxical nature of the world of the absurd, but he died a Camusian under the dark sign of the serial stamping of individuality by the demonic forces of the bureaucratizing forces of The Thing. The Camusian self ends in revolt and the possibility of solar thought investing itself against the polar night; Sartre culminates in a paralyzing sense of nausea. Neither thinker may have resolved the divided consciousness and divided politics of the Cartesian self, but their gamble with the riddle of History opens up for us a precious gap of impossibility. Indeed, now that we live in the dark times prophesied by Camus's lament for Europe in ruins, the times intimated by the fading away of the Sartrean self, that gap of impossibility created by the magnificent failure of Sartre and Camus is exactly the starting-point for all of contemporary French thought. The unsolved riddle of Camus's "absurd" and Sartre's "The Thing," which are emblematic intimations of the possessed individual as the dominant subjectivity of the postmodern condition, form in the end as in the beginning the gravitation-point for the successors to the unfinished legacy of Sartre and Camus as they begin anew the myth of History. This time, however, not under the sign of particular historical waves of political fascism, but in the presence of something perhaps much more forbidding—the actual exteriorization of the human mind into a rhetoric machine that speaks the language of technology only as seduction. Sartre and Camus may have gone to their deaths with the knowledge of the impossibility of the political division between solar thought and The Thing, but contemporary French thought begins with the suddenly problematic character of difference itself, with, that is, the essential postmodern insight that in the midst of the roaring dynamo of the technological mastery of social and non-social nature, even political resistance now works to confirm the power of a world of virtual technology which functions by the principle of alterity, by the imminent reversibility of *all* sign-functions.

Technology and the French Mind

Contemporary French discourse does not really explore the "geneal-ogy" of technological society. That is the intellectual province of the Germans from the still unthought dyad of Kant and Hegel to Nietzsche, Heidegger, Gadamer, and Habermas, with their collective reflections on the complicity of technology and the will to power, and the triumph of the will to technological mastery of social and non-social nature under the sign of nihilism. Here, Nietzsche's *On the Genealogy of Morals* reads as a psychoanalytics in advance of the coming to be of passive and suicidal nihilism, with its repertoire of conscience-vivisection and body-vivisec-tion, as the majoritarian opinion of the fully matured phase of techno-logical society. In the German mind, cynical reason is thought to its bitterest roots in what Pietr Sloterdijk has described in *The Critique of Cynical Reason*, as "enlightened false consciousness."[8]

Where the French mind excells, and brilliantly so, is in describing, almost unself-consciously, the aftermath of the implosion of the techno-logical dynamo as the language of mastery of social and non-social nature. In their collective imagination is rehearsed the terminal symptoms of the age of technology triumphant: the death of politics, the death of aesthetics, the death of the self, the death of the social, the death of sex. What we witness in contemporary French discourse is a report, all the more uncensored for its theoretical, yet cynical, innocence of its entrapment in the language of technology, of the fate of subjectivity in the postmodern condition, that is, the age when the will to technique achieves its aestheticized point of excess. Study the French mind, then, as a grisly but seductive description of possessed individualism in the terminal phase of technological society, that phase where technology actually comes alive in the form of eating space, eating culture, and eating time. Here, the legacy of Camus's "absurd" and Sartre's "seriality" comes alive again in evocative descriptions of the fully possessed subject of technological society: sometimes possessed by the imminently reversible language of seduction (Baudrillard); sometimes possessed by technolo-gies of cynical power tattooing the flesh and colonizing the imaginary domain of psychoanalytics (Foucault); sometimes possessed by cynical rhetoric without a subject (Barthes); and sometimes possessed by the strategical language of a dromocratic war machine (Virilio).

Indeed, the Sartrean self may have finally faded away, but what remains in the French mind is a series of cold abstractions: Baudrillard's "simulacrum," Lyotard's "driftworks," Virilio's "chrono-politics," and Foucault's "technologies of the self." Here, no remembrance of the historical self intervenes between the French mind and its unrelieved theorization of the mediascape. What we witness, instead, are direct uncensored reports from the wiping clean of the horizon by the seductive language of the mediascape. A passive, inscribed subject, then, enucleated within the horizon of a technological dynamo that speaks only in the language of seduction and affirmation. Catastrophe sites actually, theo-rized by a French mind that can function so brilliantly because it is itself a catastrophe theorem.

Not technology as an object which we can hold outside of ourselves, but technique as *us*, as a grisly sign of the possession of body and mind. Thus, Baudrillard explores the seduction of the simulacrum at the level of power; Barthes develops a rhetorical strategy for understanding the sign games of invisible technology; Foucault writes a theory of bi-modern subjectivity under the sign of cynical power; Lyotard explores technology at level of a libidinal economy of power; and Deleuze and Guattari draw out the delirium and paranoia of life after the desiring-machine.

What emerges from the French account of technology is an image of the individual as a *bimodern minotaur*: a technically constituted self which is both a condition of the preservation of, and a constitutive justification for, technological society. Heidegger once talked of the terminal phase of technology as involving the harvesting of social and non-social energy. The French discourse on technology, which is in its key impulses a discourse on possessed individualism, describes in detail the actual method of this Heideggerian vision of technology as a harvesting of subjectivity, speech, language, action, and desire. Before the contemporary French account of technology, it was still possible to talk of a horizon beyond technique. After their writings, the horizon finally closes and we are left with the terrible knowledge of even transgression itself as proving only the impossibility of overcoming the limit experience. We are left, that is, with an unsettling awareness of the possessed individual as the emblematic sign of subjectivity in the time of the ecstatic twilight of technological society.

The Classical Moment in French Thought

More, perhaps, than we may suspect, contemporary French thought is a brilliant reprise of a more ancient quarrel among three classical attitudes towards existence: pragmatic naturalism (Virilio, Lyotard, Deleuze and Guattari, Foucault), Lucretian fatalism (Baudrillard and Barthes) and Epicurean sensuality (Irigaray). These philosophical impulses commonly respond to the question of what are we to do in the midst of technological society, when technology is no longer an object that we can hold outside of ourselves but now, in the form of a dynamic will to technique which enucleates techne and logos in a common horizon, is itself *the* dominant form of western being—possessed individualism. Possessed, that is, to such a point of hysteria and excess that the memory and rules of possession are forgotten and, indeed, are mistakenly taken up as the possibility of human agency. In the French mind, there is no agency, no subject capable of appropriation, no acquisitive self, only a possessed subject which exists with such intensity that it disappears into its own simulacra. The seduced subject, the disciplined subject, the purely decadent subject, the subject as a seductive game without purpose, the subject as pure speed, a war machine: that is the fatal insight of French thought, with this improvement, however. Not body possession for any strategical purpose outside of itself, but in pure indifference. Possessed individualism as *the* condition of modern freedom, because it involves perfect forgetfulness: of history, of sexuality, of the memoried self.

It is this zone of the possessed individual which is the common focus of the awakening of the more ancient debate among naturalists, Lucretians and Epicureans in the French mind. The Lucretians in French thought (Barthes and Baudrillard), having no restraining sense of historical agency or dialectics, describe in brilliant detail the dark charm of technology as seduction, a game of chance and probability, without beginning or end, in which we float as spectral impulses within the smooth and unbroken surface of the mediascape (Baudrillard) or within the acquired organicity of technology as a rhetoric machine (Barthes). This perspective is fatalistic, but not tragic, since it does not have the requisite sense of the irony of experience or the lament for absence which would add the tension necessary for tragedy. A blank fatalism without expectation of relief, the Lucretian strain in French thought has the great, but ultimately fatal, merit of exercising no *différend* from that which it purports to study. From Baudrillard's inscription of the Borgian surrealistic logic of the labyrinth into the language of seduction to Barthes's making of himself a "degree zero," a point of self-cancellation and self-implosion, within the machinery of cynical rhetoric, the Lucretian impulse in the French mind can be so replete with insights into technological society because it is actually the most advanced stage of technical consciousness. A perfectly parasitic theory which, entering the body of the technological host, becomes immediately clonal of its deepest genetic logic. Indeed, just because the French Lucretians have entered so deeply into the nominalistic logic of technological society, they have also awoken to its nightmare. This may be why so much of the Lucretian impulse in contemporary France, just as in its classical past, ultimately ends in melancholy skepticism, from Baudrillard's fatal game of an always reversible seduction played out across the fields of political economy (*The Mirror of Production*), psychoanalysis (*L'Échange symbolique et la mort*), and media culture (*Les stratégies fatales*) to Barthes's propensity at the end of his life for the bitterness of nostalgia without remembrance. Hyper-Lucretians in the postmodern condition, the technological fatalism of Barthes and Baudrillard are often accused by their detractors of a lack of historical specificity. But this criticism entirely misses their central insight that in the terminal history of the cynical sign, only the virtual world of technical culture is materialized, and only those cultural codes coming under the sign of a cynical rhetoric are imminently reversible, and thus always put in play in cyberspace. While melancholy skepticism and political stoicism may have the obvious demerit of not providing instant relief from technology as degeneration, they have the saving grace of not short-circuiting into a modernist materialism which, for all of its militant appeals for historical specificity, blindsides itself to the hyper-materiality of virtual technology—cyberspace—as the new religion of the postmodern scene. Saved by their melancholy fatalism from the historical burden of providing a happy ending to their stories of the *stratégies fatales*, Barthes and Baudrillard are finally liberated to play the game of seduction to its end; that is, to make of their writing a theatre of the cynical sign, always reversible, always simultaneously fatalistic and utopian, always paradoxical, ironic, and fatally doubled.

Pragmatic naturalists are just the opposite. Adapting to a cultural materialism either because of their nascent Christianity (Virilio), resurfaced Kantianism (Lyotard), or their discovery of a new revelatory moment in Spinoza's ethics (Deleuze and Guattari), the strain of pragmatic naturalism in French thought rejects the inward bitterness of melancholy skepticism for a politics of cultural resistance. Here, the full oppressiveness of the dynamic will to technological mastery of the social and non-social universe can be felt in blood, just because it is viewed from the counter-perspective of the will to resist and to transform: Lyotard's *différend*, Virilio's critique of the actual fascism of dromocratic consciousness; Deleuze and Guattari's "thousand plateaus." Because their images of the technological dynamo are cut across the grain of political remembrance, this perspective succeeds in detailing the historical specificity of technology as degeneration, and of fulfilling once again

Gramsci's admonition for optimism of the will against the most immovable of objects. Of course, the transformative political will which motivates this perspective should not be discounted because it remains blind to its lack of success in overcoming what might be called the "Foucauldian enigma." That is, when the will to technique is invested by the logic of the cynical sign, when alterity becomes the energizing principle of a culture which feeds on the Bataillean logic of exterminism, waste and self-cancellation, then the *différend*, most of all, mutates into the bi-polar logic of a cynical power that *requires* resistance as a way of territorializing its otherwise purely abstract relationality. Ironically, it might be said of the naturalist perspective in French thought what Augustine once remarked of those other secular pragmatists at the eclipse of the Roman empire, that their best hopes would ultimately be dashed against the rocks of the very naturalism that they thought would save them. Thus, Lyotard may provide a searing theorization of the deconstruction of human subjectivity in the technological sensorium, but his best hopes for "refusing the honour of the name" by means of the *différend* finds its naturalist denouement in his panic search for a new Kantian regulator.[9] Even Virilio who has transformed the understanding of technology into a brilliant analysis of the "aesthetics of disappearance" retreats to the new "bunker archeology" of religion.[10] That the pragmatic naturalist strain in French thought is ultimately doomed by the very assumptions that make it possible, does not diminish its historical importance. In the tradition of the Camusian refusal of Germanic ideology on behalf of Mediterranean solar thought, French pragmatism is also in the way of an entanglement with the absurd, a gap of impossibility which, if it ultimately does not heal the wound which its analysis exposes, has the merit of refusing a sutured thought and a sutured political practice. It succeeds politically because of its profound intellectual failure.

Abuse Value

In the theatre of the contemporary French mind we witness how the advanced outriders of the western mind choose to think of themselves at the end of the millennium. We see theorists who make of their reflections an agency of abuse value, for running across the text of cynical power and of bringing to the surface of consciousness its energizing principle of alterity; that is, the aimless flipping of the postmodern scene between inertia and speed, between terminal aesthetics and the memoried self.

This is not to claim that contemporary French writers are conscious of being theorists of technological society. Baudrillard traces out the privileged signs of seduction; Foucault theorizes the trajectory of impossibility of transgression; Deleuze and Guattari focus on a libidinal economy of desire; and Barthes writes eloquently of the empire of the sign. And indeed, they are not theorists of technology in the narrow sense of the term, as tools, but in the most comprehensive sense of the term as the meeting of techne and logos under the sign of the will to power. What we witness in the French mind is a full rehearsal of possible life positions in the fully matured phase of technological society, when technology achieves the stage of possessed individualism. Here, Foucault can write of the self as a technology (together with technologies of production, communication, and consumption); Baudrillard can describe in grisly, but seductive, detail the flatline terrain of the cynical sign of the mediascape; Barthes, escaping the classical rhetorical legacy of the speaking subject, describes technological society as an oratorical machine, where rhetoric is the language of power of the postmodern body as a war machine. Virilio, the theorist par excellence of speed and politics, writes from the end of technological society, at that point where technology implodes into inertia, appearing to speed up because it is undergoing a great inertial drag towards an infinite slowness.

Indeed, a full description of the key psychoanalytical impulse of possessed individualism—bimodernism—is to be discovered in the French mind. No longer modernism with its endless reprise on the historical tradition of the great referents, and certainly not a social realist reading of postmodernism (for in the French mind, we are dealing less with the intensification of modernism than with an entirely new cultural phenomena). What is the bimodern condition? It is the contemporary human situation of living at the violent edge of primitivism and simulation, of an indefinite reversibility in the order of things wherein only the excessive cancellation of difference through violence reenergizes the process. The bimodern condition, then, as a time of excessive tendencies towards violent boredom and suicidal nihilism: driftworks between ecstasy and terminal catastrophe. Here, the horizon finally closes and we are left with the fatal residues of all the referents in the ecstasy of ruins. That fatal moment prophesied by Heidegger's reflections on the technological logic of the death camps as the genetic logic of the bimodern scene. And all this under the sign of seduction.

The French discourse on technology explores terminal culture with such violent intensity that it is replete with significant images: Baudrillard's simulacrum, Barthes's empire of the sign, Lyotard's driftworks, Virilio's war machine, and Deleuze and Guattari's "rhizomes" as a scene of the sado-masochism of cynical power. If these thinkers have none of the historical agency of Sartre nor the tragic remembrance of Camus, that is not to diminish their understanding of technological society. For in their writings are to be discovered uncensored reports on the aftermath of historical decay. Thus, Baudrillard shows how the logic of seduction undermines all established systems of meaning; Foucault writes of the constitution of the fictious bourgeois ego by a cynical power; Barthes demonstrates the sovereignty of power which functions as a rhetoric machine, where myth implodes into the dark logic of the cynical sign. While contemporary French discourse may not provide visions of human emancipation, it does have the merit of describing the evolution of technological nihilism up to its stage of simulation, and, thereupon to the age of sacrificial culture, in addition to theorizing the internal dynamics of technology under the sign of cynical power. These are theorists of possessed individualism in whose respective writings are to be discovered the psychology, ethics, media strategies, and ontology of postmodern subjectivity; i.e., the possessed individual. Here, the dynamic language of mastery of social and non-social nature finally comes inside, and takes possession of (our) bodies and minds which welcome it as a form of freedom.

2

PAUL VIRILIO:
THE POSTMODERN BODY AS A WAR
MACHINE

> We are passengers of the empty circle who only wish to arrive before
> they leave. Speed is a perfect will to impotence.
> Virilio, *Speed and Politics*

Virtual Technology

Someday it might well be said that the political history of the late
twentieth century, the fateful time of the *fin de millennium*, was written
under the sign of Paul Virilio. For in his theoretical imagination all of the
key tendencies of the historical epoch are rehearsed: the creation of the

postmodern body as a war machine; the fantastic acceleration of culture to its imminent moment of collapse in a nowhere zone between speed and inertia; the mutation of subjectivity into "dromocratic conscious-ness";[1] the irradiation of the mediascape by a "logistics of perception"[2] that work according to the rules of the virtual world. Virilio is, in fact, the emblematic theorist of the end of the modernist phase of technology, that historically specifiable period when it was still possible to speak of a division between technique extrinsic to human subjectivity and the interior world of imagination and sensibility, and the appearance of virtual technology. Technology, that is, which boards the body as a "metabolic vehicle",[3] exteriorizes its capacities from speech and memory to eyesight, and then replicates the human sensorium in a mediascape that actually comes alive as a virtual being with its own intelligence (dromocratic intelligence), power (the speed of movement), logic of perspective (the dromoscope of the media), and biological rhythm (the war machine which functions according to the threefold logic of tactics, strategy, and an endless preparation for war). To read Virilio is to *know* technology as a dark vampiric logic which, much like the schizoid figure of Leland/Bob in David Lynch's *Twin Peaks*, takes possession of the human body as its inhabiting spirit. He is, perhaps, the world's first virtual theorist, the writer who seeks to understand the universe of technology and politics, not by standing outside of its violent logic, but by travelling inside its deepest interstices with such speed, such "appar-ent" theoretical force, and such insistent moral concerns that the virtual world of technology is finally compelled to disclose its secret, to finally say that "real power is not knowledge-power or the accumulation of wealth, but 'moving power'...speed is the hope of the west."[4] In Virilio's theorization, we leave behind the old universe of competing ideologies, entering into the 'new world order' of dromology. Dromology? That's the empire of *immediacy*: speed and communication where the self mutates into a classless cyborg, half-flesh, half-metal, where living means quick circulation through the technical capillaries of the mediascape, where culture is reduced to the society of the spectacle, and where power is generalized in the form of the predatory logic of the war machine.

But then, Virilio is a myth-maker of the world of virtual technology. In his work, we see them all: a more fundamental moral struggle between subjugated human knowledge and a menacing dromocratic intelligence flashing across all of the screens and networks(*The Aesthetics of Disappear-*

ance); the "jet subjectivity" of the vacant bodies drifting across the airport terminals of the world(*Speed and Politics*); the "exhausted offence" of the dictatorship of movement (*Pure War*); the disappearance of politics into the terminal phase of the "logistics of perception" (*Cinema and War)*; and the transformation of cityscapes into an architecture of war, complete with mutant bodies caught up in an endless drift through all the circulatory capillaries of the transportation network. This is one theorist of technology who reaches back to a more classical understanding of the intimations of deprival released by technology as degeneration in order to recuperate, in the imagination if not in practice, an epochal tension between the labyrinth of domination of everyday technological life and the subjugated knowledge of a "possible" human experience outside the technical maelstrom. Acting under a more ancient philosophical impulse, Virilio actually writes an *epic* of technological experience, with lament as his chosen form of meditation.

The Postmodern Body as a War Machine

There is a robotic performance installation by the artist Tony Brown, which describes perfectly the cold cybernetic universe of Paul Virilio.

Entitled simply *Two Machines for Feeling*[5], the installation consists of two robotic figures, one a *Metropolis*-like cyborg whose chromium arms move through a repetitive sequence of motions, and the other a small porcelain ballerina whose magnified pixel-image is projected onto a white screen enclosed in a protective plexiglass box. While the cyborg is programmed by an invisible computer secreted in the corner of the installation, the ballerina image is attached to a cyclotron which whirls the screen with violent intensity. When the power is turned on, the cyborg robot begins to move in gestures of a purely mechanical signature, while the ballerina moves with such acceleration that the pixle image begins to mutate: a degendered ballerina and an ironic cyborg trapped as the brilliant stars of a performance without performers.

This sculptural installation shows us on the outside what we have become in the inside in the era of virtual technology. It is a 1990s version of the almost surrealistic mirror-reversals, time warps, and space shifts of *Alice in Wonderland*, except this time, rather than slip from the Real into the fantasy world of a deck of cards come alive, in *Two Machines for Feeling*

Tony Brown, *Two Machines for Feeling*

we actually enter into the dark semiological interior of information society. In a culture that is pulverized by the mediascape to the extent that we can now speak of neon brains, electric egos, and data skin as the bigger circuitry of a society held together by the sleek sheen of surface and network, entering into the simulacra of *Two Machines for Feeling* is something akin to being positioned in the hallucinogenic world of postmodern technology. It is like space travel in the society of the super chip, where, however, we become passive observers of what is happening to us in the complex sign-system of information society. *Two Machines for Feeling* is, in fact, a perfect simulacra of a culture modelled on pure speed; one which is driven from within by the reduction of experience to dromocratic consciousness—with us, this time, as dangling schizoids in the postmodern body as a war machine.

Two Machines for Feeling is insightful as a Virilo-like analysis of the complex inner discourse of postmodern technology. This artistic production is, to begin with, about the "virtual body," which does not exist except as an empty site for the convergence of the great axes traced by three discourses: the digital coding of a technical culture which is programmed by computer-generated logic (the micro-computer in *Two Machines for Feeling* controls the mechanical actions of the cyborg and the sequencing of the ballerina's image-system); the implosive logic of the image reservoir (this is a perfect image of television with the pixel image as the Real and we as the missing matter of the production); and the imminent violence of the cyclotronic ballerina (Brown says that "narrative continuity in information society can only be assured by a violent speeding up of the dynamo"). As a semiology of the postmodern body as a war machine, *Two Machines for Feeling* is perfect: it is all gender slippage (the cyborg has no sex; and the ballerina has no objective existence except as a tiny porcelain doll—the production is about degendered, virtual sex). It is all technologically dependent (as in performance art when you turn off the energy supply and the technical apparatus dissolves into instant ruins). Everything here plays at the edge of the ecstasy of speed and the detritus of inertia; a psychoanalysis of war machines where "fascination turns into psychosis." And this architectural installation forces to the surface the ideological inscriptions hidden in the formal structure of technology (the visual continuity of the dancing ballerina can only be maintained by the flattening of the image, and us with it, at warp speeds); and we are ideologically positioned as inert observers of the spectacle of velocity in ruins.

Indeed, *Two Machines for Feeling* is the world's first culture smasher, as violent as the centrifugal motion of the cyclotron in the atom smashing of particle physics as it whips around elementary particles until they achieve escape velocity. It combines optics, cybernetics, robotics, and industrial centrifuging into an exact simulacrum of how *power as speed* functions today. And what are the elementary *social* particles that are whipped into an endless free-fall from this violent and hallucinogenic act of culture smashing? They comprise the *social* itself as the dark missing matter of the new universe of communication technologies. In the end, *Two Machines for Feeling* is about the death of the social and the triumph of the postmodern technology of pure speed as a war machine, one in which we are all processed as its mute encryptions. A violent world of what the military like to call N(uclear), B(iological) C(ontaminants)—machine talk in which we are all captured.

Speed Fetishism

The loss of Material Space leads to the government of nothing but
time...The violence of speed has become both the location and the
law, the world's destiny and *its destination*.

Virilio, Speed and Politics

All of Virilio's work is like *Two Machines for Feeling*. In the same way
that Brown explores the inner grammatical codes of technology as violent
speed, Virilio actually *writes* the empire of speed. In his writing,
technologies of subjectivity undergo a fantastic acceleration, to that point
of terminal velocity where what remains is a spectral space—the disappeared body trapped in a twilight zone between inertia and a violent
psychosis of speed. Indeed, Virilio does not simply theorize the relationship of speed and power or, for that matter, speed and art; his writerly
imagination *is* speed. If he can finally say of himself "I work in
staircases,"[6] it is because his general cultural strategy is to travel in hyper-
reality with such abandon that his theoretical imagination becomes a
simulacrum of that which it seeks to describe. To read Virilio is to become
aware simultaneously of the investiture of culture, and of one's own body,
by the threefold logic of technology as a war machine; by, that is, a
dromocratic logic which functions according to a tactics, strategy and
lengthy preparation for war.[7] Here, Hume's early warning that science
inscribes itself now in the flesh finally comes alive in Virilio's understanding of a fatal acceleration of culture under the sign of a dromocratic
war machine. This is, finally, a theory of *eating time* (chrono-politics
where the floating body of Howard Hughes becomes the emblematic
"metabolic vehicle" for a society which drifts in an always specious
present); of *eating space* ("In this precarious fiction, speed would
suddenly become a destiny, a form of progress, in other words, a
civilization in which each speed would be something of a religion in
time"[8]); and of *eating bodies* (as in particle physics, all that counts now is
"the speed of the moving body and the undetectability of its path"[9]).
Speed fetishism is the key psychoanalytics of the society of cyborgs.

So then, three theses on the fetishism of speed: speed power, speed
war, and speed flesh.

Speed Power

Not content to simply expose the terminal need for speed as the basic code of cyborg culture, Virilio has done something different and more difficult. Like a hyper-Hobbes of the twentieth century, he has written a postmodern *Leviathan* for technological society in an advanced stage of decay and decomposition. Just as Hobbes projected the general principles of the Newtonian physics of the modern age into a general theory of the power field as operating under the contractual principles of ruthless competition mediated by the sovereign spirit of the Leviathan, so too, Virilio transposes onto the screen of postmodern culture a theory of political domination based upon the principles of elementary particle physics. In Virilio's political theory, all the scientific terms of quantum physics come alive as historically specific descriptions of the ideology of technological liberalism: a society of "brownian motion," bodies as "abstract vectors of speed," the government of "chrono-politics," a "dromology" of speed. Just as Hobbes understood immediately that the discrete "interactional" universe of Newtonian physics was less an objective description of an external nature than an ideological projection of the dominant myth of *modern* social nature; Virilio also assumes that quantum physics mirrors the ruling myths of *postmodern* social nature. With this difference, however. While Hobbes's *Leviathan* ultimately finds its means of political settlement in the alienation of individual property rights to a common sovereign for purposes of collective order and security; Virilio's *Leviathan* has no existence other than an alien, abstract, almost demonic, "goverment of time"—a postmodern *Leviathan* which, operating as a vector of time and sight, governs a world which has decomposed into a culture of "super strings," that is, into a dark mass which implodes with all of the final brilliant density of flashes, quarks and red dwarfs. Here, power undergoes such a massive acceleration that it finally shatters into the exploding universe of the abstract control of the dimensions of time: the harvesting of political, body, labor, and sex time.

It is just because Virilio theorizes power under the sign of postmodern quantum physics that his thought is so replete with brilliant insights into speed as the privileged, but violent, vector of the state sector. Thus, Virilio on postmodern government states:

> The Ministry of Time sketched in each vector will finally be
> accomplished following the dimension of the biggest vehicle there is,

the State vector. The whole geographical history of the distribution of land and countries would stop in favor of a single regrouping of time, power no longer being comparable to anything but a "meteorology".[10]

The reality of power in this first modern state appears beyond the accumulation of violence as the accumulation of movement. In short on July 14, 1789, the taking of the Bastille was a truly Foucauldian error...the famous symbol of imprisonment is an empty fortress, with no one to liberate (except the Marquis de Sade, *ed.*)[11]

For Virilio, power now begins on the other side of the Foucauldian error and of what might be called the mercantilist distortion. Refusing both "knowledge-power" and "commodity-power", rejecting, that is, both the reduction of power to the monisms of epistemology or economy, Virilio theorizes the disappearance of power into a vector of speed. Here, power is only knowable, not as a form of coercion, nor as a knowledge-vector, nor as a strategy of accumulation, but as a certain form of violent mobility, a logistics of fractals in which the hologram of the whole can be seen only in the indefinite miniaturization of the dispersed subject. Consequently, if he can claim that "there is no industrial revolution, only a dromocratic revolution; no democracy, only a dromocracy; no strategy, only a dromology,"[12] it is because, more than most, Virilio approaches Nietzsche in understanding the dynamic language of the "will to will" as the architecture of the power field, across which subjectivity is splayed. Or, as Virilio states in *Speed and Politics:* "The related knowledge of knowing-power, or power knowledge, is eliminated to the benefit of moving-power—in other words the study of tendencies and flows."[13] Which means that in a way more *politically* radical than Foucault's "relational" theory of power, Derrida's "surplus," Baudrillard's "seduction," or Lyotard's "refusal to honour the Name," Virilio has written the world's first purely *circulatory* theory of power—power as a terminator vector of violent speed.

Speed Wars

It is probably due to Virilio's understanding of the deep entanglement of speed and war that he can be so politically radical on the question of power. In focussing to such a great extent on the war machine, Virilio theorizes a zone of violent movement which, if it possesses such a low epistemological profile, has a surplus of strategic significance. Here,

Virilio is the French Clausewitz: a theorist who, working in the spectral terrain of the late twentieth century, analyzes the "tendencies and flows" of the war machine to discover its underlying *tactics* ("the intelligence of the hunt"), *strategy* ("the logic of politics") and *logistics* (where "war is less about actual episodes of war, than about lengthy preparations for war"; or, as Virilio quotes the Pentagon: "logistics is about the transferal of a nation's potential to its military machine").[14]

As the theorist who has first discovered the perspectival terrain of 'virtual' war, Virilio is unrelenting in his analysis of war as a hybrid form of possessed individualism. Consequently, he can say: "Dromocratic intelligence...is not excercised against a more or less determined military adversary, but as a permanent assault on the world, and through it on human nature."[15] Here, we pass beyond "this war of movement of mechanized forces, (to) reach the strategy of Brownian movement, a kind of chronological and pendular war that revives ancient popular and geographical warfare by geostrategic homogenization of the globe."[16] Indeed, if Virilio speaks with such a historical sweep of the entwinement of speed and war, it is due in no small part to the fact that his political diagnosis of the times is based, not simply upon a philosophy of history, but upon a *metaphysic* of military history. Indeed, Virilio's metaphysics parallel Nietzsche's conclusions in *The Will to Power* concerning "suicidal nihilism" as the inevitable psychological fallout from the dynamic spirit of willing which, knowing that there is no substantive purpose to its willing, would "rather will *nothingness* than *not* will."[17] The parallels are direct: the exterminatory nihilism of Nietzsche's "will to power" is replicated by Virilio's "dromocracy"; Nietzsche's "ascetic priests who work to alter the direction of *ressentiment*" anticipate Virilio's "warrior priests"; Nietzsche's "maggot man" is substituted by Virilio's description of the parasited body as a "metabolic vehicle"; Nietzsche's "nowhere" of the "noonday sun," populated by those living in a post-catastrophe time after the "wiping clean of the horizon," grounds Virilio's image of the endlessly circulating body of the social mass drifting in perfect polar inertia between past and future; and, finally, Nietzsche's power as an empty "perspectival simulacra" is the metaphysical basis, the "grammatical error," for Virilio's theorization of virtual power as a "sight machine".

Indeed, if there can be such an apparent convergence between Virilio's metaphysic of military history as the triumphant blast of dromocracy and Nietzsche's will to power, it is because Virilio's thought represents a practical manifestation of Nietzsche's grim diagnosis of the coming storm of technological nihilism. The spirit of sacrificial violence which pervades Nietzsche's thought comes alive in all of its dread in Virilio's discussion of the spirit of "endocolonization": the war spirit, that is, which finally liberated of any political or religious limit, colonizes time (a nowhere space), the city (a nowhere place), history itself (a nowhere genealogy), and clonal bodies (as empty "boarded vehicles"). Writing one hundred years after Nietzsche, at the end of the twentieth and not the nineteenth century, Virilio *is* the truth of Nietzsche's prophecy. Indeed, it might even be suggested that *The Will to Power* and *Pure War* are the beginning-and end-points of the twentieth century. Nietzsche's meditation on nihilism was written at the dawn of the last cold days of rationalism, when, as Camus has said, murder (in the name of justice) and reason (in the spirit of the hope of historical dispensation) were still ambivalent partners, but partners nonetheless; and Virilio's reflections on the sacrificial violence of the war spirit was written in the aftermath of a century of the slaughterhouse. One became the dark prophecy of a philosopher of the darkness within; the other a fragmented, and often interrupted, survivor's report on the bitter political truths contained in that prophecy. The former a historical prognosis that the "conscience-vivisection" of the spirit of ressentiment would ultimately give rise to "ascetic priests" who would alter the direction of resentment by providing sacrificial scapegoats, including the infirmities of one's own body; the latter a philosophical disquisition, written in the literary form of military cyberpunk, on the externalization of the revenge-seeking spirit of ressentiment into the universal homogenous state of dromocracy.

In the same way that Nietzsche could write so well of the darkness to infinity within the emergent bourgeois spirit because he was the most excessive practitioner of ressentiment; so too, can Virilio understand dromocractic consciousness, because his texts are actually little war machines: violent speedways which deconstruct everything in their path, from subjectivity ("polar inertia") and flesh ("bodies without wills") to class struggle ("dromocratic consciousness") and warriors ("perverted priests"). Virilio's war spirit can take its place on the stage of contemporary political history with such triumphant energy, because it sums up in one brilliant theoretical concept—dromology—the double sign of presencing and absence, which is surely the epochal consciousness of the postmodern condition. Here, the will to dromocracy, to the bestiary of "bodies without wills" possessed by the exterminatory logic of the war machine functions according to the principle of "alterity": putting into presence the restless "will to will" so eloquently prophesied by Nietzsche and Heidegger as the "perspectival simulacra" at the disappearing centre of cynical power; and eliminating from the human condition the varied forms of remembrance, from that of bodies with wills to time and history. Here, dromocratic intelligence is the form which cynical reason takes in the age of enlightened false consciousness. The dynamic mastery of social and non-social nature in the language of technological willing, in the name of the freedom of the greater conveniences, is a bestiary for all those "bodies without wills." Consequently, dromocratic intelligence consists essentially in "eating the globe" (the investiture in nuclear strategies of deterrence), "eating politics" (where politics must be overcome by the war machine precisely because the political implies limits on the will to will), "eating bodies" (all the "civilian soldiers" become dromocratic holograms), and "eating time" (the dromocratic world is that of "chrono-politics" and fractal space where the possessed individual is infinitely permeable as a "metabolic vehicle" demanding to be pirated). Or, as Virilio states, dromocracy can find its moment of cyclical completion in the coupling of "Holy War" and the "Just War," that moment when the "warrior of the Holy War and the technician of nuclear war" discover a common surcease in sacrificial violence. *Pure War* then, as a "circular voyage," with no specific beginning or definite ending, but only the terminal violent velocity of the death of power and the death of history as the signs of fading epochal consciousness.

Speed Flesh

> What is to be feared, what has a more calamitous effect than any other calamity, is that man should inspire not profound fear but profound *nausea*; also not great fear but great *pity*. Suppose these two were one day to unite, they would inevitably beget one of the uncanniest monsters: the "last will" of man, his will to nothingness, nihilism.
> Nietzsche, *On the Genealogy of Morals*

Nietzsche's meeting of nausea and pity—the will to nothingness—takes place at the constitution of Virilio's "dromocratic subject." Here, the body is emptied out, turned into a blank "metabolic vehicle," a speedway absorbing all of the infrared signs of the mediascape, trapped in a closed horizon which moves according to technological, not biological, time. Virilio is explicit about the interpellation of the flesh by speed or, what is the same, the interiorization of the "will to nothingness" as the dynamic subject of dromology. A new kind of body has now been created: "the presence in the world of bodies without wills."[18] The metabolic body is always ready to be invaded by all of the war strategies: sometimes by psychiatry, sometimes by Skinnerian behavioralist strategies of operant conditioning; sometimes by advertising campaigns which translate a Kleinian object fixation into moments of seduction and abandonment. And sometimes too, by direct acts of political piracy:

> Depending on the time and latitude, the multitude of bodies with no souls, living dead, zombies, possessed, ... is imposed through all history: a slow-motion destruction of the opponent, the adversary, the prisoner, the slave; an economy of military violence likening the human cattle to the ancient stolen herd of the hunter- raiders...In total war, the Nazis will do nothing different when they create an internal social front against the foreign bodies of the Jews, gypsies and Slavs. The deportation camps are but the laboratories in which the cattle are treated industrially—put to work in the mines, on logistical worksites, subjected to medical or social experiments, the ultimate recuperation of fat, bones, hair...[19]

> Its absolute inhumanity was but the ostensible reintroduction of the history of the originary bestiary, of the immense mass of domestic bodies, bodies unknown and unknowable. What else has the proletariat been since antiquity, if not an entirely domesticated category of bodies, a prolific, engine-towing class, the phantom presence in the historical narrative of a floating population linked to the satisfaction of logistical demands?[20]

Not just the "originary bestiary" of the death camps, but the extension of "bodies without wills" into the class physics of the working population: the proletariat ("industrial drones"); middle-class professionals pursuing private careers (frenzied "war machines" engaged in a great forgetting); our historical leaders (floating bodies trapped in polar drift—

the embodiment of the "will to nothingness"). Two great classes of bodies, then: predators and parasites. Virilio's predators are the "war-rior/priests" who name the site of the sacrificial table of values, and whose function as abuse value is to violently reenergize the field. And parasites, from dromocratic specialists to the "industrial drones" of the war machine, who can be motivated by the will to nothingness because their bodies are already "technical prostheses," always in flight, driven by extreme anxiety, and motivated by a vision of freedom which is measured by the lowered standard of the "petty conveniences." Two "originary bestiaries" then: the *social* bestiary of the Fascist and Communist death camps in which Heidegger's prophecy concerning the mass extension of the exterminatory logic of the "harvesting" of surplus living energies is historically validated; and the *cultural* bestiary of late capitalist societies where the "silent majority" can be so celebrated because it is the triumph of Nietzsche's "last man"—the "maggot man" in the twilight time of cold rationalism where assassins in judge's cloaks are already slipping away to commit murder in the name of justice; and where all the passive nihilists can be heard sighing in revenge: "Someone or other must be to blame for my feeling ill."[21] In the cultural bestiary, the body is pulverized and splayed apart, like a "lap dissolve"; a traveller in time where from the viewpoint of the advanced cybernetic technologies of the mediascape, the body is always a big failure in desperate need of supplementary technical prosthetics. Not designer facial surgery any longer, with its skin, cheek augmentation, and forehead lifts, but now the creation of new techno-heads for all those Hollywood stars—the advanced outriders of dromocratic society; and not skin any longer, but cyber-flesh, skin without memory and without history, for the body whose destiny is that of a pulsating war machine; and not even emotions, but libidinal *mood implants*—New Age spiritualism—for the decayed, but never healthier, body of the "last man." Nietzsche's last man, therefore, as the leading citizen of dromology: the "body without will" which can be the locus of the accumulation of movement, of pure speed, because it is now only a technical servomecha-nism. The body has become the "silent majority" which can be penetrated easily by the war logic of the "need for security" and "deterrence" because slave morality is its key psychology—that is, sadism against the weak, and servile masochism in the presence of authority. Speed flesh, then, for "bodies without wills" in a war machine which functions on the basis of a biological logic, and which projects the psychology of the "last man" into all those drifting "metabolic vehicles," waiting to be boarded by the mediascape.

Dromocratic Aesthetics

> What are war machines? They are machines in reverse —they produce accidents, disappearances, deaths, breakdowns. I think war in this sense conveys something which we are experiencing in peacetime: the accident has now become ordinary.
>
> Virilio, *Impulse*

> It is reality we have to measure in a cinematic way.
>
> Virilio, *War and Cinema*

Virilio can write so eloquently about the implosion of experience into "speed spaces"[22] because he is above all a theorist of aesthetics. Not of aesthetics in relationship to art or high culture, but of a more materialistic order of aesthetics: the aesthetics of war, the violent aesthetics of the "sight machine," the aesthetics of cinema as a colonizing apparatus. In Virilio's discourse, the question of aesthetics departs forever from the privileged region of the sublime, becoming something rubbed deeply by the warring languages of the dromocracy. Indeed, in his thought there has been the unwavering elaboration of a single brillant *aperçu*: that, today, aesthetics is the topological site of pure power, and that, consequently, to contest the hegemony of cynical power one must struggle materialistically, which is to say aesthetically. This double strategy informs *L'horizon négatif* (an elaboration of the aesthetics of "speed-space"), structures the internal analysis of *The Sight Machine* (a vectoral description of the colonization of perspective), and keynotes *War and Cinema* (cinema as the reality-principle of the war machine).

Virilio is deadly serious about the dominations and power of the sight machine. If we live in the era of the empire of space (and the disappearance of time), it is because the western rationalist eschatology has inscribed itself by means of a twofold political strategy: by the policing of the imminent codes of perspective, and by the ideological constitution of the viewing subject, the bourgeois ego, as the triangulation point of politics, culture, and society. An optical reality, therefore, which can so easily careen away from the signifiers of a time-biased culture (context, history, materiality) because it is all about illusion. The reinscription, that is, of the old world of temporality, of duration, of felt bodies, into a new architectural space: the virtual space of illusional perspective, of the seduction of the ruling image-repertoire.

This insight into the entwinement of aesthetics and power in the western regime lends Virilio's analysis tremendous dynamism, range and intellectual charisma. For example, it enables him to encompass in a single theoretical discourse a critical exploration of the aesthetic colonization of subjectivity, the enfolding of cinema within the war machine, strategies for policing visual experience, and the inevitable existential fallout—the flipping of "speed-spaces" between acceleration and inertia. Here at last is a thinker who grounds his cinematic theory in a broader philosophical understanding of the genealogy of the sight machine, who actually *materializes* aesthetics in a historically specific theory of the strategic alliance of cinema and war technologies, and who writes dramatically about the entwinement of aesthetics and power as a crash scene of escape velocity and fatal inertia. A dromocratic aesthetics which flips randomly between full throttle forward and full thrusters reverse as its principle of motion, and collapse.

All of Virilio's work is informed by an aesthetics of insurrection. He begins *L'horizon négatif* with a discussion of the imperialism of perspective (doubles), and how for him two plus two always equals five just as much as form plus content equals absence. "My designs, my paintings were attempts to interrogate the interstices of vision...I refused categorically the privileges of perception."[23] But, of course, if Virilio had simply remained an aesthetic rebel in the artistic domain of painting and design, that would make of his work only a romantic refusal of, and thus deep assent to, the governing logic of the sight machine. A machinery for policing visual experience which has always relied on the privileged figure of the aesthetic rebel to re-energize the flagging energies of the optical apparatus. What makes Virilio different, and what gives his writing such a fascinating sense of originality and urgency of political critique, is that he is one aesthetic rebel who goes all the way. A philosopher of the optic nerve of power who magnifies an early central insight concerning the enfolding of speed, vision, and power into an epic of *our* disappearance into the cinema of war.

Writing with the steady hand of a thinker who has had the good intellectual fortune (but bad political luck) of having really existing history confirm the essential accuracy of his theoretical analysis in his own lifetime (*War and Cinema* is a postmodern bible of the Gulf War), Virilio leads us directly into the "interstices" of dromocratic aesthetics as the real world. Everything is there. Not just *War and Cinema* as a theoretical diagnosis in advance of technological strategies of the "New World Order," but of something even more significant. No longer cinema as a mediated, and thus distanced, representation of war, but the reverse. War *as* cinema. And this in the most deeply materialistic sense.

> There is no war without representation: no sophisticated weaponry without psychological mystification. Weapons are tools not just of destruction but also of perception —that is to say, stimulants that make themselves felt through chemical, neurological processes in the sense organs and the central nervous system, affecting human reactions and even the perceptual identification and differentiation of objects.[24]

Viewing "the history of battle (as) primarily the history of radically changing fields of perception" and theorizing war as "scoring territorial, economic or other cultural victories as in appropriating the 'immateriality' of perceptual fields,"[25] Virilio recodes the history of contemporary warfare under the sign of cinema. Here, the target has become a "cinema location," the field of battle "a film set out of bounds to civilians," the movement of mechanized forces gives way to a "strategy of Brownian motion, a geostrategic homogenization," and the very nature of war planning disappears into 3-D computer graphics, like "animated cartoons or flow charts." A new world of "cinematic derealization" for the radical immateriality of the war machine as a visual vortex of the logistics of perception. In this strange new world, war commanders are confronted with the strategic problem of the "third window," that is, "how to light the surrounding world without seeing it."[26] And, of course, the solution is purely sociological: to construct a telematic panoptic complete with new inventions such as the "light intensifier," "low-lighting television," "photogammetry," "the photon accelerator," "thermographic pictures" that define objects by temperature, aerial drones, sensors capable of providing a continuous flow of telemetry about smells and movement.[27] Real-time observations, then, for a war machine that works only in the visual language of radical immateriality.

In Virilio's world, the war machine as a "speed-space" is always typified by a fantastic extension of the technical means of visual telemetry accompanied by a big drop in the actual "human relations" of warfare. On this point, Virilio is emphatic. If "cinema could be hijacked by war," then the subjects of the war machine could quickly vanish into a chrono-photographic sphere of speed and communication.[28] Consequently, the war machine is a fatal scene of "pure inertia:" a doubled sign of speed-up and inertial drag.

> Burying beetles are always present at the foundation or re-establish-ment of military states. And if *memory is science* for those who make war, the memory in question is not like that of popular culture based upon common experience: rather it is a parallel memory, a paramnesia, a mislocation in time and space, an illusion of the *déjà vu*. The state's only original existence is as a visual hallucination akin to dreaming.[29]

"Cinematic derealization" invades all the privileged signifiers of the war machine when it goes on automatic. And nothing more so than the rapid decomposition of the warrior's personality: "tied to his machine, imprisoned in the closed circuits of electronics the war pilot is no more than a motor-handicapped person temporarily suffering from a kind of possession analogous to the hallucinatory states of primitive warfare."[30] Consequently, the war machine runs on empty like a spent reactor: paramnesia, not collective memory; cyber-bodies, not human subjectiv-ity; a technology of visual hallucinations, not embodied optics; cold digital violence, not hot conflict.

Virilio understands so clearly the aesthetics of war because the war machine has now disappeared into its own field of immateriality. Not vanished in the form of a final catastrophe or of a long-anticipated big bang, but disappeared in a more desultory, virtual manner. Maybe the war machine does not exist anymore except as a melancholic referential sign of its own disappearance. In this case, a *sociological* hypothesis: the war machine can be automatic since its presence is required as a fatal scene of the attempted recuperation of symbolic exchange, a *mise en scène* for the failed return of primitivism to technological society. And the war machine exists because its probable effects are not those of cataclysm, but of dissuasion and indefinite illusion. In the latter case, a *poetic* hypoth-esis: the war machine as a scene of "cinematic derealization": a strategy for masquerading the normalization of virtual war as a kind of non-event, a massive technological gridlock. At least, for example, that is what Baudrillard claims in his recent challenge (and assent) to Virilio's account of the aesthetics of war.

> Discussing with Paul Virilio our opinions on this war, diametrically opposed, the one convinced of an escalation leading to apocalypse, the other towards dissuasion and an indefinite virtual war, we have concluded that this war (the Gulf War) decidedly stems from, and moves in two directions at once. At this time the programmatic escalation of war is implacable, and its non-happening is also inevitable—the war moves at the same time towards the two extremes of intensification and dissuasion. [31]

Maybe Virilio's writings on war and cinema can attract such universal fascination because there is no longer a relationship between cinematic technology and war. No longer the hijacking of cinema by war, but now the hijacking of war by cinema: a relentless will to subordinate war to the logistics of optical phenomena. What if war was not an automatic machine but a crash modulator, if war strategies had already flipped beyond the gathering of telemetried information to the nightly struggle of algorithmic functions, if cyber-war no longer performed according to the optical requirements of the screen but to the fractal imperatives of the hologram, and if war was now nothing but a purely mathematical equation floating in competing computer systems? What if war actually was like Nintendo where real time, real information, and real telemetry did not matter in the least. We are finally in the era of virtual war, an N-dimensional war machine that operates in the space of illusion, and functions according to pre-established algorithmic values. The war becomes a matter of digital information, which itself has only the status of an algorithmic hallucination. In this case, the relationship of cinema and war would be similar to the movies: a nostalgic reprise to a time when power could still be discussed optically, when audiences could be constituted sociologically, and when the technology of the camera would allude to the later presence of telemetried sensors as eliminating a theatre of operations governed by mechanical forces. Just because Virilio forces a subordination of war to the optical rules of sociology, he may have missed the real trompe l'oeil involved in the aesthetics of war: the vanishing of war into the perspectival simulacra of digital illusions. The violence of the war machine only confirms the disappearance of war into a perfect simulation.

Intimations of Deprival

If Virilio can stand so clearly opposed to most of contemporary French thought, it is because in his thought a larger eschatological contest is at play: one which pits the moral suasion of the religious imagination against the will to nothingness of secular dromocracy. Clearly out of step with his intellectual times, but as definitely in tune with the deep religious sensibility in French thought, Virilio invests the ethical refusal of the Christian thinker against the power field of the war machine. Indeed, in much the same way as Karl Jaspers noted in *Man in the Modern Age* that the "radical crisis" finds its furthest point of expansion in the individual who says *no*, Virilio inveighs with religious dissent against the fully rationalized society of dromocratic technology. Here, Virilio's turn to Christianity provides him with an ethical focus for his critique of technology ("I have always been interested in missing things...people, time, history"[32]); with a focus of recuperation (recovering time against space-binding technologies); and with a method—the more ancient one of lament.

As a deeply religious thinker, Virilio continues anew a tradition of Christian dissent in French thought which successively marks such cultural philosophers as Jacques Ellul, Teilhard de Chardin, and Etienne Gilson. Indeed, Gilson once noted that the Catholic imagination often runs parallel to the leading cultural discoveries of the time, precisely because the epistemology of Thomistic Catholicism, with its stress on discovering moments of "aesthetic apperception" and, consequently, laying the foundations for new "technological epiphanies," parallels in theory and in deed the privileging of aesthetic experience in late modernist societies. Thus, Teilhard de Chardin could create in his writings an ecological paradigm of human experience in which events stand in the balance between the materialism of the biosphere and the noosphere, requiring for their dynamic unification a cultural aesthetic in which a new universal community of human imagination would provide a dialectical reconciliation of biosphere and noosphere into a fused ecological whole. And even more to the point, the Catholic dissent of Jacques Ellul can enjoy such global appeal as an ethical critique of technological society, because Ellul recuperates a value-driven ethics of remembrance and refusal against the "technological imperative." In Ellul's "no" to the technological imperative, there is simultaneously a *presencing* of the dynamic will to technological mastery in areas ranging from politics and economy to the media and sexuality, and an intense listening for intimations of deprival which might remind us of what has been lost in the coming to be of the technological dynamo.

Virilio is like Ellul to this extent. They both have recourse to a form of religious dissent against technological society, which is as notable for the originality of its methodological assumptions as for its ethical judgments. Which is to say that Virilio, like Ellul, works to bring into presence the very worst that can be thought or imagined of technological society. While in Ellul's case, this amounts to a highly systematic, and devastatingly coherent, theory of the operations of the "imperative to technology" as the deepest postulate and practical manifestation of the technological dynamo, for Virilio this results in a daring retheorization of technology under the sign of *virtual optics*: of dromocratic technology in its most mature aesthetic phase. In addition, while Ellul works the real material terrain of the technological imperative to renew the long-suppressed question of ethics and technique, to ask, that is, the ethical consequences for culture, labor, and social practices of the instrumental imperatives of technology; Virilio thinks in terms of "absences" (of history, time, and people) so as to foreground the exterminatory ethics of the entwinement of speed and the war machine. But, of course, while Ellul's thought ultimately remains encrusted within the epistemological terrain of modernism, theorizing as it does a clear difference between technology and ethics; Virilio's theory of technology is more ambivalent, ironic and paradoxical. That is because Virilio's opening position is different: his is not a modernist, but a postmodern discourse on technology, one which begins with the invasion of the body, with the "endo-colonization" of subjectivity, by the "last will" of technique and which culminates in a text like *The Sight Machine* with the exteriorization of the human sensorium into a virtual machine that, in finally acquiring organicity, has also allied itself with the life-functions of the preservation of the (techno)species.

Curiously, the religious dissent so favored by Virilio finds its deepest philosophical, and ethical, counterpart in the thought of the Canadian theorist, George Grant. While beginning from strikingly different national traditions, that of post-revolutionary France with its commitment to Cartesian rationalism and of pre-revolutionary Canada with its propensity for moral refusal leavened by *ressentiment*, Grant has followed an intellectual journey similar to that of Virilio. In books ranging from *Lament for a Nation, Technology and Empire*, and *Philosophy in the Mass Age* to *Time as History*, Grant has translated a Christian refusal of the language of technological mastery into an epochal statement on passive and suicidal nihilism.[33] He is the North American thinker whose meditations brush the closest to Nietzsche's meditations on the "will to will" and who, moreover, makes of his encounter with Nietzsche and Heidegger a sweeping diagnosis and ethical condemnation of technological liberalism. Here, Grant's eloquent, but grim, reflections on passive and suicidal nihilism as the twin psychology of majoritarian opinion in the American empire of technology fully approximates Virilio's dark perspective on "bodies without wills"; and if Grant can trace the fatal strategy of technological liberalism to the "civilizational contradiction" immanent in its Kantian heritage, then that is to anticipate Virilio's analysis of the existing radical division in virtual technology between the exterminatory (perspectival) logic of the "sight machine" and the "disappearing" of subjectivity, bodies, and history. If Virilio resists the hegemony of space-binding technologies by an appeal for the recovery of a sense of embodied time, it is only to repeat what Grant has earlier said in *Time as History*, where the recuperation of time, of historical consciousness, is made the great counterpart of Nietzsche's understanding of cynical power as a "perspectival simulacrum."

There is no indication that Virilio is acquainted with the writings of George Grant, and this is a pity. Not the least for Virilio, whose thought would benefit from familiarity with Grant's philosopical leavening of the question of technology and justice; but also for those engaged in thinking through the "civilizational contradiction" of the technological eschatology. Grant went to his death unable to solve the Kantian dilemma. Unable, that is, to resolve a problem that all his thinking on technological nihilism led him almost inevitably to pose, but which, ironically, because of the very ethical assumptions underlying his pattern of thought, made him singularly ill-equipped to resolve. In Grant's account, Kant's recourse to the "morally good will" (morality as a fact of reason) to which we are recommended by virtue of obedience is a necessary, but futile, attempt to brush over the radical division of the western mind: the division, that is, between the preservation of a more ancient account of justice and the unlimited (technical) freedom to be found in the "will to make one's own life."[34] Following reluctantly, and with a full sense of dread, but *following* nonetheless Nietzsche's pronouncement of Kant as the "great delayer", Grant nominated the key civilizational contradiction of technological society to be just this radical diremption in the western mind between the reality of technological secularism and the irreality, in an age which is relativist and historicist, of preserving the absolutes of the old morality. As Grant recounts, in his critique of the liberal account of justice:

> He delayed them from knowing there are no moral facts, but only the moral interpretation of facts, and that these interpretations can be explained as arising from the historical vicissitudes of the senses. Moral interpretations are what we call our 'values', and these are what our wills impose upon the facts.[35]

In Grant's estimation, technological society is plagued from within by the "great darkness" ensuing from the knowledge, in the midst of the necessity and chance of contemporary science, of being able to recur to a more ancient account of justice; while being unable to forget the question "of what it means to say that justice is what we are fitted for."[36] Which is to intimate that we, the survivors of the post-catastrophe of the Kantian dilemma, live in that impossible division, between the enucleation of the horizon by the technological "will to nothingness," and the remembrance of an account of justice that can only be thought in the language of technical willing, as an "ethical value" so impugned by Nietzsche as yet another "condition of preservation." Now, I have privileged the contribution of Grant to an understanding of technological society as a more measured way of making the point that Virilio's religious dissent is simultaneously the singular strength and fatal flaw of his perspective. It is his strength because, beyond the inscribed skepticism of Baudrillard, and in a *rupture* more striking than Foucault's redoubling to excess of the "limit experience" or Derrida's "spurs," Virilio is the one

French thinker who laments absence. In his thought, an ethical recourse to absence is raised to a level of political dissent and ethical critique, all the more remarkable for its general rarity in the intellectual scene. Indeed, Virilio can write *The Aesthetics of Disappearance* because all his texts have focussed on "absented" subjects: from the absented city of *Bunker Archeology* and the absented bodies of *Speed and Politics* to the absented (human) vision of *Cinema and War* and *The Sight Machine*. If Virilio can think with such poetic eloquence and political passion about absented history, it is the political reward for his deliberate turning back to a more ancient religious account of justice, all the more politically persuasive for its lack of theological articulation in his thought. Nevertheless this is also the fatal weakness of his perspective because, like Grant before him who said that in the end he could not accept Nietzsche and so turned back to the certitudes of Christian faith, Virilio never solves the civilizational dilemma of the "morally good will." Indeed, it might be said that Virilio's vision of technological society *is* the morally good will in full force. There is simultaneously a hyper-critique of the nihilism of the war spirit at work in the politics (social contract theory), in the ideology (instrumental activism) and in the ethics (improved utilitarianism as bourgeois common-sense) of technological liberalism; and an ennobled moment of remembrance of the "absences," first marginalized, then exterminated, by the technological dynamo. That Virilio does not provide an ethical means of resolving the impossibility of "thinking justice" within technology, or of transgressing the closed horizon of dromology, does not diminish the importance of his theoretical oeuvre. His lasting importance as a philosopher of speed may be, in fact, to show clearly the limits and possibilities of pragmatic naturalism in the postmodern condition. The limits in the sense that, like his classical predecessors in the Greek enlightenment, Virilio's seminal concept—the dromocratic state—must of necessity result in a historical sterility: a social totalization which, precisely because of its absence of thought about the civilizational contradiction of the Kantian dilemma, *cannot* be thought outside the closed horizon of a technological conception of justice; and which, moreover, because of its ethical inability to think technology as seduction *will not* countenance the possibility that the virtual technology of the "sight machine" is always acceptable to the last man as the emblematic form of freedom, the final reconciliation of justice and technology.

(Technologically) beyond his time because he is so (ethically) behind his time, a primitive Christian in a cyber-Rome, Virilio's recourse is to the ancient method of lament. A lament for the loss of politics:

> For Baudrillard, the disappearance of politics is positive. For me it is totally negative.
>
> I don't believe in explanations. I believe in suggestions, in the obvious quality of the implicit. Being an urbanist and an architect, I am used to constructing clear systems, machines that work well. I don't believe it's writing's job to do the same thing. I don't like two-and-two-is-four-type writing. That's why, finally, I respect Foucault more than I like him.[38]

A lament, ultimately, for the violent suppression of a measured vision of the *good qua good* in the name of cynical power: "As a Christian, I do the opposite. I say no. It's the abomination of desolation. On the contrary, we have to turn back in the name of a belief that death doesn't exist, that there is an afterlife, we must not only refute Holy War, but the notion of a Just War."[39] Or as Grant, Virilio's true counterpart in the New World, in, that is, the continent where the dialectic of European enlightenment was first practically realized as its autochthon, has said:

> Our present is like being lost in the wilderness, where every pine and rock and bay appears to us as both known and unknown, and therefore as uncertain pointers on the way back to human habitation. The sun is hidden by the clouds and the usefulness of our ancient compasses has been put into question. Even what is beautiful—has been made equivocal for us both in detail and definition.[40]

But then, Grant died an unrepentant Christian and a political Straussian. And perhaps one day it might be written of Virilio that, like a larger community of religious thinkers before him, including Grant but also extending to Ellul and Etienne Gilson, the Christian turn in his thought meant that he could not finally follow Nietzsche in understanding cynical power on its dark side, where it mutates into the ambivalent sign of seduction. That point where the cynical power of the dromoscopy would suddenly exhibit a fascinating moment of imminent reversibility: all speed, all inertia; all crash aesthetics, all lament for justice absented. Here, dromocratic culture is just what Bataille intimated: a violent imposition, and the deepest language of freedom. Baudrillard called this paradox "seduction," Foucault spoke of a "power without roots," Bataille spoke of "excess," Barthes talked about a fatal "sign slide," and even Lyotard, more pragmatic than most, intimated the inherent reversibility of experience. But, of course, this would be to say that dromology is *both* decay and freedom; and thus to admit to the necessary reversibility of radical skepticism and justice as alterities in human experience. It would also be to claim that dromocratic violence and the will to justice are flip sides of the same sign system, and to agree with Bataille that no one has ever really been interested in coherency, that dromocratic violence can be so seductive because of its privileging of self-cancellation, self-exterminism, and self-disappearance. Here, Bataille's "excess" would be Virilio's "speed"; that point where the dromocratic war machine would be theorized as operating under the schizoid signs of seduction and abandonment. That Virilio cannot go this far does his perspective no dishonour. He is, after all, a theorist of a more classical stamp, one who would forsake the moment of creative regeneration provided by sacrificial violence for the sake of maintaining a line of demarcation across the vicissitudes of human experience. In the end, with and against Kant, he insists on the impossibility of thinking justice within the horizon of technical violence. That his vision of dromocratic politics can be so deeply original in theorizing the invisible, virtual horizon of the sight machine; that he has so much to say about the war spirit as the dynamic language of possessed individualism, may imply that, like the priest who has lost his faith but still dispenses it to others in a final gesture of sacrifice, Virilio's exercize of the "morally good will" makes of him the last and best of all the saints.

Cultural Excursus I: The Mohawk Refusal

It is appropriate to reflect on Virilio's *Pure War* in the context of Montréal, a city which in the early 1990s was the scene of the violent application of the Canadian war machine against its aboriginal population, the Mohawks. A city, that is, which in the summer of 1990 experienced as part of its cultural politics the invasion of the Mohawk reservations surrounding Montréal by all the policing strategies that could be produced by the state: 6000 soldiers of the Canadian army, complete with tanks, armoured personal carriers, and even TOW missiles, the greater part of the Quebec provincial police, and the RCMP. All of this array of power belonging to the state was set against, in the end, less than 50 Mohawks who only wished to prevent the destruction of a sacred pine grove of their ancestors by developers intent on extending a golf course to eighteen holes. (In a perfect Virilian gesture, the Mohawks not only reclaimed the sacred pine grove at Oka, but also took physical control of the Mercier Bridge—one of the main traffic arteries between the south shore suburbs and the island of Montréal.) If in cultural politics we should be able to read the universal in the particular, to decipher a larger war logic in local applications, then Oka is Pure War in Virilio's sense.

First, it is about an urban space, not as a site of commerce, but as defined in relation to war. That's Montréal, which has always been a site of war first, and of commerce second. A city of two founding exterminisms: the original genocide of aboriginals by French colonizers who, speaking the language of Christian salvation, imposed the spatial logic of "enlightenment" on the northern tier of North America; and then the attempted exterminism of the local French population by English colonizers, for whom the "conquest of Québec" was most of all about suppression of a Catholic French America by a Protestant mercantilist logic. Montréal, then, as a Virilian space: an intensely urban zone as a spatial vector for the war machine: a site of maneouvre, negotiation and conquest—a violent scene of sacrificial power.

Second, in the summer of 1990 Oka is a matter of tactics, strategy and, most of all, logisitics. Just as Virilio has theorized in *Pure War*, it is about an indefinite preparation for war, involving the colonization ("endocolonization") of local populations. Thus, for example, the Canadian military stated that this "conflict" could be over in two or three minutes, but the real war was a "media war" to win over the consciousness of the civilian population. Here, logistics could be an endless preparation for war: control of food, communications, space. And all of this accompanied by constant armed helicopter flights over Montréal as if to demonstrate symbolically the state's control of the local population. Is this not what Virilio has described as "state terrorism"—the act of war without a declaration of war, so that there is no formal protection of civil rights, and no political rights for international agencies to intervene on

Oka, Quebec 1990
Photographs: Linda Dawn Hammond

Oka, Quebec 1990
Photographs: Linda Dawn Hammond

behalf of the Mohawks? And is the indefinite occupation of Oka and the ceaseless police raids into other aboriginal territories not an indefinite preparation for war in another way: not really about the Mohawks at all, but a violent warning to all the First Nation peoples, most of all to the Cree in Northern Quebec, not to intervene physically (by blocking roads) or legally (by court actions) in the future construction of James Bay II, the Great Whale project (the state-driven plan for a vast extension of hydro-electrical development on aboriginal lands in Northern Quebec)? Oka, then, as a pure technological war between the energy requirements of the high-intensity market society and the irrepressible demands of aboriginal peoples for control of their territory and culture. A technological war, that is, where the war machine has come inside of us and taken possession of our identity. Virilio is correct: "All of us are already civilian soldiers. We don't recognize the militarized part of (our) identity, of (our) consciousness."[41] And anyway, what is so dangerous about the Mohawks, about the sovereignty claims of the First Nations? Virilio states that the war machine is the crystallization of science as the language of power, of the depletion of the energies of society, and their draining away into the war machine. Maybe this is what is so threatening about the struggles of the First Nations. It violates and refuses the genetic logic of the technological dynamo.

Consequently, a politics of remembrance of twenty-five thousand years of aboriginal history verus what Virilio describes as the extermination of time (in favor of a purely spatialized power) in technological societies. Here, real tribal consciousness and real grounded sovereignty— duration and a vital sense of sedentariness—militate against the pure mobility of the war machine. And not just memory, but the cultivation of a dynamic ecological relationship with land, economy, and culture on the part of the Mohawks now stands opposed to the disappearance of territory into abstract vectors of speed in consumer culture. This is perfectly captured by the bitter political struggle between the peoples of the First Nations of Labrador and NATO over low-level training flights by fighter jets. In Virilio's war machine, it is always land without history, people without remembrance, space without a sense of duration, the abstract control of territory against the loss of history of territory.

Finally, what makes the Mohawks really dangerous for the Canadian state is their creation of a model of democratic politics based on matriarchal principles of rule. Here, the traditional form of the Longhouse society militates against rule by the technocratic specialists of the war machine. Virilio says that in the war machine, there are no longer any priests who could mediate death. Now, the leaders of the war machine can speak triumphantly of mega-deaths, because death is also total release from the earthly constraints of gravitation. In this sense, the Mohawks are like gravity, a fall into real time, whose very communal existence militates against the pure speed, the will to endless circulation, of the war machine. If the peoples of the First Nations can be so oppressed, not only in Montréal but also in all of the Americas, from the United States to South America, maybe that is because they are the bad conscience of what we have become in the society of speed and war: perfect sacrificial scapegoats for feelings of anxiety and doubt about that which has been lost in the coming to be of the technological dynamo.

Cultural Excursus II:
The Gulf War as the World's First Virtual War

Not a hot war, but a new form of cold war. At least in its first phase, fought with cruise missiles that are heat seeking, but which themselves give off no traces of heat; seen not with normal ocular vision but with optical scanners which magnify star light from the cold depths of outer space, filled with surgically green images of laser guided missiles with fighter pilots themselves telematic spectators to their own acts of destruction. A scopophiliac war fought without depth, always on the surfaces of the screen and the network, and always under the sign of the ecstasy of catastrophe.

This is not a war of association, but something radically different. What the American psychologist, Robert Jay Lifton, has said is the first war typified by the generalized neurosis of "dissociation"—radical distancing— between anachronic viewers and the material consequences of the bombing. First, the mental dissociation of weapons from their virtual operators in the form of jet fighter pilots, who were reported flying into combat listening to heavy metal music, with *Van Halen* as the band of choice. Second, the dissociation of the dark and missing matter of the TV audience from the material history of the war. An informational war which was presented in its opening stages as one with no political history, no casualties, no sound, only the fascinating video games of laser-guided bombs. An image dissociation between war and its social consequences that was so complete that even cruise missiles became boring. Three "mach" is too slow, and already the army has to think up new promotional ruses to reawaken interest in an always censored media coverage. The problem, then, of "re-enchanting the simulacrum" in the Saudi desert.

Really, the Gulf War was a war of disappearances. The disappearance of the civilian population of Iraq, vanished by a perfect complicity between the Pentagon (who did not want images of the bodies of Iraqi civilians to ruin the cerebral sublimity of "The Plan," and the Iraqi military who immediately wrote off their own population as a casualty of war). The disappearance of the mass media who could proclaim loudly that this was the first of the all-TV wars, because it was the first war in which the mass media were completely shut out, forced into the role of second-order simulacra. The disappearance of American public opinion, this under the guidance of George Bush who proclaimed that "this won't be another Vietnam," because the military opened a second, and very real, front of war, a liquid war for public opinion which was overwhelmed by a violent and seductive assault on all the rhetorical signs of American martial valour.

A final war in which as Virilio has said in *Pure War* there is a conjunction of the Holy War (of religious fundamentalists) and the Just War (of nuclear technicians). A war which can be fought at the geographical meeting-point of the Tigris and Euphrates Rivers as if to emphasize that this is an epochal drama: the imminent reversal of the always forward-looking logic of the West, back to its primal origins in Mesopotamia. A religious war between the dromocratic war machine, the most intensive expression possible of the rationalist eschatology of the West, and, in however distorted a form, the "Other" of Arab nationalism.

The world's first purely designer war: a promotional war machine which scripts the whole metastasis of violence as an advertising campaign for the technological invincibility, and thus political necessity, of the "new world order."

3

_____

"Why Should We Talk When We Communicate So Well?" Baudrillard's Enchanted Simulation

Sacrificial Meditations

To begin: two paintings by Attila Richard Lukacs—*Call Michael* and *Like That*—which are a perfect simulacrum of Jean Baudrillard's universe of sacrificial violence and cold seduction.

Saint Skinheads

Call Michael is the painterly invocation of de Sade's "Mass of the Dead." Not a traditional Catholic liturgy with its celebration of the

Attila Richard Lukacs, *Call Michael*. Diane Farris Gallery.
Photo: J. Littkemann

sacrifice of Christ, but the opposite: the "black mass" of the skinheads, where, as in de Sade's imaginary kingdom of pleasure, all the sacrificial signs are reversed. Candles for high mass stick out of asses, the eucharist is offered up by hands engaged in the pleasures of sado-masochism, hightops substitute for the traditional depictions of Christ's feet nailed to the cross, and even the vestments are part of a sexual orgy that never ends. A fascinating, because so deeply disturbing, depiction, then, of sacrificial burnout that always culminates in orgiastic excess.

Does this mean that Lukacs has simply reversed the black mass, substituting the obsessive rituals of sado-masochism for the public rituals of the Catholic ceremonial? Or can there be such a comfortable, and transgressive, slide between the Christian mass of the dead and the skinhead's black mass, because both perform exactly the same ceremonial function? Sacrificial acts for a "host" that has only a purely cynical presence, an empty act of remembrance for a sacrifice which never occurred? Is the skinhead parody of Catholic liturgy its fatal truth-sayer: just as de Sade's dark kingdom of pleasure was the truth of Kant's peaceable kingdom of liberalism, does *Call Michael* represent the nothingness present at the heart of Christianity: its transmutation of the body into a cynical sign of a power that had only a purely symbolic presence? Or could it be that the Catholic mass of the dead is also a truth-sayer of the skinhead mythology: *Call Michael* as a holy act of sacrificial pleasure for the sacramentalization of young boys' bodies?

Thus, this is also a minotaur painting, a point of absolute degree-zero that is so ambivalent in its interpretation because it represents that point of a fatal impossibility: the spectre of the loss, and violent recuperation, of symbolic exchange, which haunts the cold world of the code. Here, the liturgical signs of the Catholic mass of the dead can be instantly, and devastatingly, recuperated by the skinheads because they always have only a purely cynical existence as symbols of a sacrifice which has an imaginary existence only. This painting, therefore, is less of a representation of sacrificial excess, than itself a fatal scene of sacrifice: a site for the cancellation of difference, and for the creation of a liquid slide between transgression and performance.

However, to state this is to nominate a larger truth: one that would take us beyond the mass of the dead, and its transgressive re-enactment, to the possibility that the seductive rituals of sado-masochism are also the truth of Christianity. The upraised ass as an altar for high mass, the eucharist as the sacrificial symbol of the disciplined body, the constant fascination with the visual edge of nudity and ceremonial robes. Here is announced the condensation of sado-masochism, beyond sexuality, into the pleasure of the code: the code of discipline, the code of veneration, the unbreak-able code of ceremony. That moment when two thousand years of sacrificial renewal by Christianity finally discovers its animus in the excess, discharge, and exterminism of the Skinhead's High Mass of the Dead. The spectacular scene of sacrificial burnout of Lukacs's *Call Michael*, therefore, as but the faithful mirror image of the sacrifice of Christ: a point of confirmation, not transgression. And equally, of course, this is also a ceremonial painting of skinheads as the last and best of all the Christians. Just as Heidegger warned that opposites are always most deeply entangled, Lukacs's skinheads mutate into perfect Chris-tians. Just because of the deep enucleation of their transgression within the rhetorical order of the body of Christ, they might well be viewed by a later age as priests of a new holy order, that is, as nostalgic reinvocations of Christianity in ruins. Consequently, the perfect appropriateness of the call to the Archangel Michael for a new (postmodern)mass of the dead populated, this time, with Saint Skinheads.

Cold Sadism

Is *Like That* an unforgettable invocation of the rituals of sadism, or a perfect, because so nostalgic, reflection on the impossibility of sadism in the age of the disappearing body?

Lukacs's theatre of sadistic duties and pleasures is precise. Here are to be found all of the iconic visual signs: the classical setting, much like de Sade's 'Silling Castle' with its imaginary architecture of sexual obsessions; the transposition of bodies into disciplined animals, this time saddled deer; in the right tryptych, an emblematic scene of the ruins within framed by the inertness of classical art. And, of course, overlooking the theatre of sadistic delights is the famous monkey figure, both as artistic jester to society and mirror of the primitive nature of the ritual which unfolds below. An equivalence, then, between a Gothic aesthetic and the romantic figures of the costumed executioners who can, perhaps, be so recuperative of nostalgia because they play only in the old languages of discipline, punishment, and pleasure.

If *Like That* has about it a purely nostalgic quality, it is because it is already only a historical monument to the political reality of European enlightenment in ruins. If it is accurate to say with Nietzsche that Europe now lives out its dark destiny in the last days of rationalism as "nothingness," this also intimates that modern European experience was always fatally divided between an unmediated rationalism and romanticism. Rationalism because Europe is the metaphysical centre of instrumentality without signification, and romanticism since twentieth-century Europe has been a slaughter-house of ressentiment unleavened by any sustaining and coherent ethics. And so, *Like That* actually paints the damaged subjectivity that follows from the nihilism of a radically divided experience. Here, there can only be discipline as pleasure and sexuality as bondage because they are the psychological ruins that occupy the European simulacrum. A baronial room, deer antlers on the ceiling mirrored to infinity, bodies in sexual bondage: a perfectly nostalgic recuperation in the language of sexual disciplining of the European past. It is as if Nietzsche's reflections in On *The Genealogy of Morals* had been inscribed in paint:

Attila Richard Lukacs, *Like That*. Diane Farris Gallery.

...this animal that rubbed itself raw against the bars of its cage as one tried to "tame" it; this deprived creature, racked with homesickness for the wild, who had to turn himself into an adventure, a torture chamber, an uncertain and dangerous wilderness—this fool, this yearning and desperate prisoner became the inventor of the "bad conscience." But this began the gravest and uncanniest illness, from which humanity has not yet recovered, man's suffering *of man, of himself*.[1]

But if *Like That* can paint the cold seduction of the subjectivity in ruins foreseen by Nietzsche, that may be because sadism has already taken flight elsewhere. Abandoning its privileged relationship with the sign of romanticism, and its associations with sexuality, discipline and bondage, postmodern sadism has to do with discipling of the disappearing body. A *semio*-sadism which, operating in the cool but immensely violent world of an operational simulation, functions at the level of an imminent transgression of the cynical sign. Sometimes exhibiting a fetishism for the sign, and then drifting off to *amenesis* on the question of the code, semio-sadism now knows only the delirious rules of the time after the orgy. A perfectly aestheticized sadism, then, for the cold dreams of digital creatures—half-meat, half-code—who desperately require a nostalgic reinvocation of the rituals of sexual sadism as a *mise en scène* for deflecting the eye from the disappearance of Nietzsche's "bad conscience," and its substitution by the "good conscience" of telemetried being.

And so, *Like That*: not art as a representation of sacrifice, but as itself the scene of sacrificial violence. A degree-zero point for the violent cancellation of difference, where all the signs of fetishistic power mutate and dissolve into an empty combinatorial of cynical signs. Art as a minotaur figure, so fascinating because it freely exchanges the opposing signs of victim and predator; a delirious art which, working the edge of the disappearance of sexual sadism in the sign-field of semio-sadism, approximates the dissolution and cancellation of the social field.

After the Orgy

> If it were necessary to characterize the actual state of things, I would say that it is after the orgy. The orgy is, above all, the explosive moment of modernity, that of liberation in all domains. Political liberation, sexual liberation, liberation of productive forces, liberation of destructive forces, liberation of women, of children, of unconscious tendencies, the liberation of art...Today, everything is liberated. The dice are cast; and we find ourselves collectively before the crucial question: WHAT ARE WE TO DO AFTER THE ORGY?
>
> Baudrillard, *La Transparence du mal*

Baudrillard should know, because all of his writings, from the earliest critiques of the political economy of the sign to seduction, are theoretical feasts: an explosive moment of modernity in which the rationalist eschatology of the times is first revealed, and then subverted. Nothing escapes Baudrillard's liberation: historical materialism, the autonomy of the object, the terrorism of value, the operational simulation of the code, the suppression of the "world of magic, alchemy, of the primitive mind,"[2] the death of power, the death of history, the death of sexuality, the death of the media. Not so much the critical theory of ideology, but a vast teasing out of the imminent reversibility hidden in the disappearing centre of things. Baudrillard sometimes calls this the return of the primitive mind—symbolic exchange—the suppression of which is the spectre haunting the "rationalist eschatology."[3] The terms do not really matter, since what is at work in his thought is a broader cultural project: the writing of a critique of primitive reason. Intensely energetic because he is so deliriously exhausted, charming because he is so bleak, Baudrillard is the historian of a future not yet past. In his works, the fatal disintegration of the West is arrayed in all of its melancholy excess. Just like Lukacs's artistic productions—*Like That* and *Call Michael*—Baudrillard's theoretical oeuvre is in the form of a sacrifical tableau. Not a representation from afar of the sacrificial violence at the centre of western culture (that would be referential logic which Baudrillard rejects) and certainly not a mirroring of sacrifice (in the age of fractal subjectivity, Baudrillard refuses the privileging of the mirror image in favor of the hologram), but theory as itself a sacrificial act. Here, Baudrillard enacts in the theatre of the text the epochal reduction central to all sacrificial violence: the reduction, that is, of the text to a degree-zero, to a labyrinth of the minotaur, in which writing returns to its more elemental function as the site for the cancellation of all the signs: power, history, conscious-ness, and sex. Read Baudrillard, then, not as a representation *en abyme* of sacrificial power, but as the disappearing centre of the sacrificial violence repeated infinitely in the spiral of power. Baudrillard is, perhaps, Bataille's *part maudite* which returns to unmask the false sovereignty of value at the moment of its greatest triumph.

This is to suggest that Baudrillard is really the Oswald Spengler of the cyborg age. Not so much the author of *The Decline of the West* (that would privilege the finality of the referent), but the digital historian of *The Ecstasy of the Decline*. In his theoretical imagination are rehearsed the main lines of a great, and epochal, historical drama: one that is all the more ominous because its fundamental irruptions occur first at the level of metaphysics, and only later surface in open view as the violent, terminal stages of a fading culture. A fatal metastasis, therefore, in which the world is irradiated by a "viral positivity"[4]—a hyper-realism of simulation for fractal subjects—that can achieve such a frenzied point of acceleration that it finally reaches escape velocity, leaving the modernist world of material culture behind as pure epiphenomena. Here, in a big ontological flip, techno-culture is materialized—*form* comes alive—and Baudrillard is a radical empiricist studying *our* implosion in the violent semiurgy of the "rationalist eschatology."

If Baudrillard can be a radical empiricist of the new material world of techno-culture, it is because a greater, more daring, historical vision is at work in his thought. He is one thinker who might have begun his intellectual journey as a cultural sociologist in the tradition of Lefebvre's *Everyday Life in the Modern World* and Marcel Mauss's *The Gift*, and whose intellectual genealogy might be traced to its roots in an early rereading of Lukács's fateful concept of reification (*Le Système des objets*) and thereupon to a fundamental overturning of Marx's theory of commodification (in favor of signification), who might, that is, have a proximate, local intellectual history; but whose works can be so fascinating because they play at the deeper level of a dramatic metaphysical confrontation with the cultural logic of the West, with the fatal flaw that infects the positivist edifice of the rationalist eschatology. Indeed, if Baudrillard ended his thought with a critique of rationalism, with, that is, a theorization of the shift from the commodity-form to the sign-form in the era of the "structural law of value," that would have eventually assigned his thought, and quickly so, to the ash-can of history.[5] Like Sartre before him, Baudrillard's searing depiction of the culture of signification (from *The Mirror of Production* to the *Critique of the Political Economy of the Sign)* would have terminated with the exhaustion of Sartre's *Critique of Dialectical Reason*: an eloquent, but ultimately, futile appeal for the autonomization of the subject, for, that is, the securing of the solidarity of the "fused group" against its suppression by serial culture. Indeed, if Baudrillard had only teased out the elements of the rationalist eschatology, principally the political economy of *value*, common to both the politics of left and right, to Marxism as well as positivity, that would have taken him no further than the ultimately "suicided thought" of Walter Benjamin, the poet of the dialectic of enlightenment who could take his own life on the Spanish border because he was in the end the tragic writer of *no exit* between history and the absurd: the philosopher who, unwilling to abandon his deep entanglement with the law of value, could thereby not solve the riddle of the simulational order of history. Probably against his best theoretical intentions, Baudrillard supersedes the local context of his origins in French thought, achieving a rare insight into the labyrinth of history, one which accounts simultaneously for the deadening fatalism of his melancholy skepticism as well as for the brilliant *aperçus* that light up the dark horizon of techno-culture. He becomes an astronomer of the past.

What begins in the early works—*The Mirror of Production, For a Critique of the Political Economy of the Sign*, and *Le Système des objets*—as a nostalgic lament for the loss of "symbolic exchange" under the sign of the abstract totality of the "law of value," comes to represent by that epochal text—*L'Échange symbolique et la mort*—the dynamic locus of a new metaphysic of cultural history. Not dialectics or the aesthetic of "one-dimensional society" as responses to the radical semiurgy of the rationalist totality, but the deciphering in the deepest logic of techno-culture of a fatal flaw, a fundamental moment of subversion that will haunt, and *imminently* undermine, the law of value. For Baudrillard, the doom that awaits the triumph of the sign is also its point of ecstatic fulfillment: an "imminent reversibility" that haunts the rationalist calculus and that is marked by the return of the primitive as the "strange attractor" of the law of (disintegrating) value. Before *L'Échange symbolique et la mort*, Baudrillard could write about the "loss of symbolic exchange," from myth and alchemy to the religious imagination, in the traditional form of the French modernist lament for the suppression of the "savage mind" by Cartesian eschatology: Levi-Strauss's *The Savage Mind*, Durkheim's *The Elementary Forms of the Religious Life*, Rousseau's "natural savage," Marcel Mauss's nostalgia for the primitive imagination. To this point, Baudrillard remains entangled in the rationalist eschatology, whose triumphal destiny as value-form come alive can be watched with a mixture of fascinated dread (*La Société de consommation*) and theoretical critique ("Desire in Exchange Value"); but who can only think primitivism from the outside as a past suppressed by the imposition of the tyranny of the code.

> But what authorizes science in its scorn of magic or alchemy, for example, in this disjunction of a truth to come, of a destiny of objective knowledge, hidden from the infantile miscomprehensions of earlier societies? And what authorizes the "science of history" to claim this disjunction of a history to come, of an objective finality that robs earlier societies of the determinations in which they live, of their magic, of their difference, of the meaning they attribute to themselves, in order to clarify them in the infrastructural truth of the mode of production to which we alone have the key?[6]

> It is only in the *mirror* of production and history, under the double principle of indefinite accumulation (production) and dialectical continuity (history), only by the arbitrariness of the *code*, that our

Western culture can reflect itself in the universal as the privileged moment of truth (science) or of revolution (historical materialism). Without this simulation, without this gigantic reflexivity of the concave (or convex) concept of history or production, our era loses all its privileges.[7]

To this point, Baudrillard remains an "improved Sartre" with, of course, the essential difference that, while Sartre aimed for the ideal of the autonomous subject as a counterpart to serial culture, Baudrillard extolled the "primitivist" loss of autonomized subjectivity as the focus of deserialized subjectivity. Nevertheless, after *L'Échange symbolique et la mort*, Baudrillard's mind goes over completely to the Bataillean side of the sign, to excess, discharge, and waste; to, that is, the "necessity of lack," the "reversion of the loss, the gift, the sacrifice," as the possibility for symbolic exchange.[8] The intimations of Baudrillard's sign-switch from a theoretical *critic* of the "Euclidean geometry of history" represented by historical materialism, to a grand *metaphysician* of the fatal flaw inscribed in techno-culture first appears in *The Mirror of Production*:

It is directly at the level of the production of social relations that capitalism is vulnerable and en route to perdition. Its fatal malady is not its incapacity to reproduce itself economically and politically, but its incapacity to reproduce itself *symbolically*. The symbolic social relation is the uninterrupted cycle of giving and receiving, which, in primitive exchange, includes the consumption of the "surplus" and deliberate anti-production whenever accumulation (the thing not exchanged, taken and not returned, earned and not wasted, produced and not destroyed) risks breaking the reciprocity and begins to generate power. It is this symbolic relation that the political economy model of (of capital), whose only process is that of the law of value, hence of appropriation and indefinite accumulation, *can no longer produce*. It is its radical negation. What is produced is no longer symbolically exchanged and what is not symbolically exchanged (the commodity) feeds a social relation of power and exploitation.[9]

Much like an Augustine, who could survey the opposing tendencies to pragmatism (Rome) and idealism (Athens) in the secular rationalism of classical culture and discovering therein no *internal* means for the regeneration of experience, could recommend the psychology of the direct confession of faith (Jerusalem) as a way out of the dilemma; so too,

Baudrillard, working the same sign-field as Augustine but writing in the time of the death of faith in the efficacy of direct confession, could survey once again the radical "separation" of symbolic exchange and the code— "this fatality of symbolic disintegration under the sign of economic rationality"[10]—and find therein only the ominous opening up once more, in the modern as opposed to classical enlightenment, of a radical scission in twentieth-century experience. A "separation" of primitive exchange and the law of value marked, moreover, by a double suppression: an *epistemological break* typified by a rationalist eschatology —"the phantasm of science"—which denies the validity of the prehistory of knowledge in favor of the classical and rational perspective of the Renaissance; and a *linear break* distinguished by an "accumulation of knowledge," hence of truth as a final totalization."[11]

Baudrillard's main contribution to the philosophy of culture is not only to have deciphered correctly the schizoid division of rationalist eschatology and primitive exchange, but, more importantly, to have proposed a solution to the radical "separation" of the dialectic of enlightenment. A solution which, while its results are inevitably fatal for the most dynamic tendencies of contemporary culture, foregrounds sacrificial violence as the key means for the violent regeneration of twentieth-century experience. That is to say, beginning with an elementary insight into the suppression of symbolic exchange, Baudrillard performs a Copernican revolution of thought in restoring primitivism, heretofore thought from the outside of techno-culture as its suppressed past, to its *most imminent* moment of fatal completion, of excess and ruin. Not primitivism as a past long exterminated by the triumph of the rationalist totality, but as the actual destiny of the code: that is, the seduction of loss, excess and discharge, "the necessity of lack," as the inevitable, because so fascinating, point of imminent reversibility of the law of value. Dispensing with the Augustinian solution of the psychology of directly experienced faith as a solution to the problem of the divided sign, Baudrillard makes of the sign itself, actually the *cynical sign*, the internal ground for its own rationalist valorization ("the phantasm of science") and fatal implosion (the "fatality of symbolic disintegration"). After *L'Échange symbolique et la mort*, the "necessity of lack," the "reversion to loss, dispersion..." is read directly into the code of the rationalist eschatology as its dynamic principle of historical motion.

What results is a theory of postmodern society—the simulacrum as the infinite fetishization of the code—which can be so technologically dynamic because it is following the path of a fatal disintegration. No longer rationalism versus primitive exchange or the "abstract totality" of the code versus the "necessity of lack," of symbolic exchange, but the *imminent reversibility* of the code and primitive exchange as alternating poles in the sacrificial tableau of technological society. Before this fatal historical insight, Baudrillard might have been a local French thinker, sometimes a hyper-Lukácsian (*La Société de consommation*), at other times a heretic entangled in the orthodox canon of historical materialism (*For a Critique of the Political Economy of the Sign*), or even a Lefebvrian on the question of the ideolect of the "object" (*Le Système des objets*), but after its appearance Baudrillard immediately transmutes into a metaphysician of human experience. Ironically, the leading exponent of the death of history becomes a historical chronicler of *The Ecstasy of the Decline of the West*, of the fatal destiny of the cynical sign present in the mediascape (*In the Shadow of the Silent Majorities*), in power (*Oublier Foucault*), in sexuality (*Seduction*), in the political left (*La Gauche divine*), in art (*L'Effet beaubourg*), and in (fractal) subjectivity (*La Transparence du mal*).

Indeed, taken as a whole, Baudrillard's writings trace a fatal arc in which the later writings circle back to haunt and ultimately undermine the polemical critiques of the earlier theorizations: the spectre of *Seduction* with its privileging of ambivalence haunts the radical "separatism" announced in *The Mirror of Production*; *La Transparence du mal*, with its refusal of the mirror-image in favor of the hologramic subject, is the *part maudite* of the *Système des objets*; *Cool Memories* is "symbolic exchange" to the fascination with the empire of "binary functionality" described in *For a Critique of the Political Economy of the Sign*. Baudrillard's later fascination with the fatal destiny of the reversion to loss, sacrificial violence in the games of seduction is but the imminent reversal of his own entanglement, however negatively and unfaithfully, with the law of value. But why not? If Baudrillard's writings can be a sacrificial tableau, tracing out the fatal strategy that he thought he was only theorizing from a distance, it is because he is the very first of the *postmodern primitives*: the theorist who makes of his writing a tale of seduction under the cynical sign of imminent reversibility. Consequently, the irony of the theorist who, thinking he had finally overcome the limits of the historical dispensation, writes now the elemental history of the *fin de millennium* under the spell of its own cynical, and fully delirious, sign. The history, that is, of the end of history, that moment when the proto-surrealism of Borges's *Labyrinth* spirals outwards as the magical and ambivalent terrain of the "operational simulation model" that the natural cyborg, Baudrillard's version of the possessed individual, calls home. Digital dreams, then, for the end of the world.

Digital Dreams

An astrophysicist of technological society, Baudrillard explores the bleak and seductive logic of the mediascape from another planet: from the optic of the primitive postmodern who sees in the triumphal ascendancy of the culture of signification—"viral positivity"—the gathering signs of its own violent dispersion in excess, loss, and waste. In Baudrillard's discourse the elemental discoveries of early twentieth-century physics—the quick disappearance of reality and time in the quantum physics of Heisenberg and Einstein—resurfaces in the form of a social physics. Rather than project the critique of the "referential illusion" onto the natural universe, quantum physics is flipped around and made a critical cultural theory of the disappearing social mass. What Marx once accomplished at the *ideological* level in his inversion of the religious illusion, Baudrillard does at the *virtual* level in his turning inside-out of quantum mechanics, transforming its key theses into a concrete description of the real material world of the mediascape. All of Baudrillard's language is that of astrophysics, and by extension that of all the critiques of the "referential illusion" in the image-reservoir of postmodern science: from the fractals of "tricky" mathematics and the "dark missing matter" of big bang theory to the "Brownian motion" of centrifugal experiments in the physics laboratory. And for this reason. Baudrillard theorizes that quantum physics is less an objectively deduced description of the natural universe, than an ideologically constituted fiction of the social universe which, projected outwards, appears to us now only in the valorized, and *reified*, form of an abstract totality. In a curious sense, Baudrillard demythifies the phantasm of science by demonstrating how it has taken possession of our language ("radical semiurgy"), subjectivity ("fractal subjectivity"), the mediascape (cool memories now of "operational simulation models"), our vision ("the smooth and unbroken surface of communication"), and politics ("subsuicidal").[12]

In a way more sinister, because more excessive and ambivalent, than Virilio, a chilling vision emerges of the fully disenchanted world of the third millennium. The once and future horizon, that is, of the Baudrillardian scene. A coming epoch that will be polemical in its insistence on a generalized logic of affirmation (the new spiritualism) because its ruling logic drains experience of the language of seduction. Not a violent world, but cold as cruelty: one which fulfills the dark prophecy uttered by McLuhan that ours would be the age of the "exteriorization of the human sensorium;" the epoch, that is, in which the "vicious turtles" do a big flip, putting our shells on the inside and the soft insides on the exterior.[13] McLuhan's "vicious turtles" are Baudrillard's natural cyborgs: those restless inhabitants of the world of digital dreams who find themselves seduced and abandoned in the impossible perfection of technology. Virilio might well have presented us with the grisly image of "dromology"—the war machine in which our subjectivity is processed at violent speeds—but Baudrillard deepens and intensifies this insight. In the continent of "cool memories," and "seduction," there is no transgression of the limits of dromocratic consciousness; there is no différend to mark the site of political renewal. In the Baudrillardian dream machine of "terrorist rationality," of "speech without response," there is only the *need* to play the game out to its fatal destiny. Virilio's dromocracy might bracket the religious *no* of the last of all the pragmatics, but Baudrillard's objectifiable world of the code has no shadowy horizon, only a labrynthian twisting in the mutually assured seduction of ambivalence, irony and paradox. Consequently, what results is an eschatology of technological culture, one which rehearses psychosis and fascination as the twin singularities of the *code made flesh*.

Everything is there. The simulacrum takes the place of virtual reality. Indeed, for Baudrillard, we are responding to a simulation as if it were the thing itself ('the real thing'). And why not? In the simulacrum, reality itself disappears, just vanishes, and what takes its place is a mediascape infected the dynamic logic of the hyper-reality. A society of the hyper-spectacle with such intensity that the commodity-form finally breaks free of its grounding in materiality, becoming a sign-form in a circulating machinery of immaterial desires. And not a static world either, but one which can be ruled by the language of seduction: where things are only interesting when they can be flipped at terminal speed to their opposite extreme, forced to undergo a quick cycle of imminent reversibility. Cold seduction, then, for a cool hallucinatory culture of special effects' personalities moving at warp speed to nowhere.

The Technological Eschatology

Four Aphorisms on the Baudrillardian Method:

1. The Helpless Robot

There is a robotic installation by the artist, Norman White, which describes perfectly Baudrillard's universe of technological eschatology. The robot likes to sit quietly in high-intensity consumption sites, particularly shopping malls. When someone walks close to it, alerting its optical sensors, it suddenly says: "Excuse me, excuse me!" and then asks for their help. The computer-generated instructions are random, but insistent. "Move me a little to the left." "No, that's not right; how about a little more to left." "Great, how about a little to the right." Adopting a increasingly whining tone, the robot then begins to abuse its human helper, yelling at them that they are hurting him. If you continue to assist the robot, the abuse gets worse. It only stops when you actually break the sensor field by walking away from the robot. Then the "helpless robot" begins to whimper, saying "I'm sorry. Please come back. I'll behave."

Baudrillard's theory of technology is something like the "helpless robot." A writer of books in the age of video walls, virtual technology, and computer scanning, his texts sit quietly in the midst of the frenzy of the mediascape. When you enter their optical field by reading them, from *The Ecstasy of Communication* and *Simulations* to *Seduction* and *La Transparence du mal*, they immediately invade your mind like a media virus. Unlike the "helpless robot," which remains exteriorized, liberation from the Baudrillardian virus entails brain vacuuming: the mental shutdown which Nietzsche once described as the dominant activity of the "last man," from the "forgetting of mechanical activity" to surrendering

the embodied will to the "ascetic priest."[14] But, as an antidote to the
Baudrillardian virus, even that is not guaranteed, since he is a master of
the interrupted and purely gestural text: a writing that moves aphoristi-
cally, and always seeks its own subversion through a series of self-inflicted
cuts, from self-mockery and humor to the *dédoublement* of paradox, irony,
and ambivalence. The "I'm sorry" of the *Helpless Robot* has its match in
Madonna's recent imitation of the Baudrillardian mind: "I'm contradictory. So, lucky me."[15] Or, as Baudrillard has said: "Since the world drives
to a delirious state of things, we must drive to a delirious point of view."[16]
A passive aggressive text then, for a world of passive aggressive robotic
circuitry, where the mind most of all is "satellized" in permanent orbit
around all those disappearing bodies in hyper-reality.

> That is our only architecture today: great screens on which are
> reflected atoms, particles, molecules in motion. Not a public scene or
> true public space but gigantic spaces of circulation, ventilation and
> ephemeral connection.
>
> Baudrillard, *Simulations*

2. Abuse Value

A digital world, therefore, where technology no longer functions under
the sign of use-value, but as *abuse value*. Indeed, if Baudrillard's mind can
enter the technological eschatology so deeply, it is because in an age of
abuse technology—technology that functions at the edge of seduction and
violence—Baudrillard is the first of all the abuse theorists. Often
mistakenly accused of a lack of politics, he is like Heidegger's double who,
through the act of negation, remains fatally entangled in the dialectical
object of its critique. Thus, Baudrillard can speak so ecstatically about the
death of sex, the death of communication, the death of the social, and
the death of politics, because he is their moment of imminent reversibility
and violent renewal. His texts constitute the catastrophic implosion of
the law of value that immediately flips into its opposing tendency: the
reinvestment of a system drained of meaning by the charm of seduction.
Baudrillard's theory of technology is the abuse value which races across
the fields of communication, subjectivity, sex and politics, only to renew
them through a last sacrificial act of violent regeneration. His is a
constitutively political theory, written not under the sign of the order of

value, but that of the return of seduction: reinvesting symbolic exchange in a system that is dying because of its lack of symbolism. A new French Sartre, that is, for a society organized now by signification, by the radical semiurgy of the consumption machine.

3. The New French Sartre

Indeed, Baudrillard can continue anew the Sartrean tradition because, better than most, his thought sets out to resolve the fatal point of Sartre's failure. Sartre died with an unresolvable tension between the practico-inert and the material will to transcendence, between, that is, binary functionality and symbolic exchange. Baudrillard resolves the problem of radically divided experience by suggesting that, if this contradiction could not be resolved within the dialectical logic of enlightenment, perhaps that was because the problem was stated incorrectly. Overcoming the Cartesian legacy of French thought that always moved between the static poles of hermeticism and schizophrenia, Baudrillard sought to make of Sartre first, and then of Descartes, their own violent doubles: to introduce, that is, the imminent reversibility of seduction as the principle of technological change into a system fast-frozen in its own abstract tensions. Which is to say that Baudrillard writes in order to find the labrynthian point of imminent reversibility hidden in the order of things: "cynical power" as the alterity of panoptic power (*Oublier Foucault*); seduction as the instant reversal of the law of production (*Seduction*); the impossibility of "consummation" as the dark truth that haunts the universe of consumption (*For a Critique of the Political Economy of the Sign*); symbolic exchange as the alterity of the new cold order of communication; (*The Ecstasy of Communication*); and "viral positivity" as the fatal destiny of simulation (*La Transparence du mal*). Here, Baudrillard fulfills Sartre's project of thinking against the demonic logic of "The Thing" (Sartre's description of the disenchanted world of viral bureaucracy) by showing how "The Thing" has taken possesion of politics (*Le Gauche divine*); communication (the chilled universe of "hyper-reality"); history (the culture of "signification"); and sexuality (the disappearance of the body into a "pure simulacrum"). Consequently, Baudrillard is Sartre's twin star: the dark and missing matter of the Sartrean universe of dialectical contestation. Not the Sartre of the *Critique of Dialectical*

Reason but of the *Critique of Viral Reason*; not of *Being and Nothingness* but of *Being as Seduction*; not of *Nausea* but of the "delirious pleasures" of *Stratégies Fatales*; not of *No Exit* but of *Escape Velocities*. This is the Sartre of the order of consumption, not of production; of "symbolic surplus" as the new "fused group" in the simulational order of reality; of "primitive exchange" as the long-sought "reciprocity" for digital beings; of the "code" as "seriality" in its most intensive manifestation; of "technological abstractions" as the new hyper-domain of the "practico-inert"; and, finally, of simulation, then "viral reality," as the real meaning of alienation in data culture.[17] Writing within the historical context of the triumph of political economy, with its valorization of the law of value, Sartre could be fully entangled in a political debate with and against materialism. Baudrillard is also a materialist, but of a radically flipped order of reality, where culture now assumes autonomous materiality, and economy fades into an epiphenomenal status. Sartre might have theorized in the pre-cybernetic order of the law of value where energy (political economy) controls information (culture); but now it is just the reverse. Baudrillard writes in the cybernetic order of the "structural law of value" where information (the fatal destiny of the "sign") controls energy (the production machine).[18] Just as Sartre could speak of "abstract totalities" that achieve hegemonic status; so too, Baudrillard. In *The Mirror of Production*, Baudrillard distinguishes between the "abstract totalizations of technology" and the dark and suppressed region of symbolic exchange. Like Sartre, not content in the end to mount a theoretical and political critique *external* to the object of his reflections, Baudrillard enters directly into the image-reservoir of technological society as its abuse value. Beaming back the mirror of seduction against the "mirror of production," Baudrillard is that side of the Sartrean mind that finally comes alive as a viral invader of techno-culture: a theorist, that is, whose texts are themselves holograms of "viral positivity" in which the part enucleates the logic of the whole. Baudrillard's Sartre is the bad destiny and hyper-conscience of the age of digital dreams.

4. The Mirror of America

Baudrillard began his theoretical reflections with a critical review of the work of Marshall McLuhan as the very first of his publications because McLuhan is his fatal destiny. After all, what else is the Baudrillardian universe of hyper-reality but a fantastic extension and speeding-up of the exteriorized mind in telematic society, prophesied in all of McLuhan's writings. Indeed, if Baudrillard, writing in *The Mirror of Production*, could chide McLuhan for his "enthusiasm" for the technological totality, it would only be an ironic foretaste of the political criticism that Baudrillard himself would later receive from those who would claim that he is too deeply, and enthusiastically, inscribed in the supposed object of his critique—the mediascape. The theoretical similarities are obvious: Baudrillard's simulacrum is McLuhan's processed environments; McLuhan's "prosthetic culture" where we become servo-mechanisms of the technology is an exact description of Baudrillard's speaking Japanese cars:

> One can think of the car as no longer an object of performance, but as an information network. The famous Japanese car that speaks to you, that "spontaneously" informs you of its general state and of your general state, possibly refusing to function if you are not functioning well, the car as deliberating consultant and partner in the general negotiation of a lifestyle, ...communication with the car itself, (as) a perpetual test of the subject's presence with his own objects, an uninterrupted interface.[19]

If Baudrillard can write with such eloquence about the fantastic piling up of dead power in all those disenchanted systems that refuse participation in the "spoken word," which seek political control by denying the counter-gift of "reciprocity" in communication, it is only a latter-day reflection on McLuhan's famous lament for the loss of "oral culture" with the triumph of spatializing technologies. And if McLuhan could think of technology as disease, it was anticipatory of Baudrillard's later reflections on the cold universe of digital technology as a form of viral contamination, or *evil*, that takes possession of subjectivity, making of it the site of a fantastic proliferation of cynical signs, like a cancer cell. Here, the exteriorization of the central nervous system in the mediascape which McLuhan predicted finds its moment of historical completion in Baudrillard's theorization of hyper-reality. Consequently, if Baudrillard could note that the "schizo is bereft of every scene, open to everything in spite of himself, living in the greatest confusion,"[20] it is but an afterimage of McLuhan's observation on the fate of subjectivity in the digital world:

Electromagnetic technology requires utter human docility and acqui-
escence of meditation such as now befits an organism that wears its
brains outside its hide and its nerves outside its skin.[21]

There is such a deep affinity between Baudrillard and McLuhan
because in a strange intellectual twist McLuhan is the last of all the
Europeans, while Baudrillard is the first of all the Americans. Just as the
violent founding of technological society as the primal of the North
American mind represented the playing-out across the wilderness of the
Americas of the fatal dialectic of European enlightenment, the new post-
1993 Europe is formed under the sign of the dialectic of American
enlightenment: that is, under the cynical sign of technological liberalism.
McLuhan fully realized the European ancestry of technological society,
which is why so much of his thinking about technology was self-
consciously formulated in relation to classical antiquity. Thus, for
example, McLuhan's "new method of study," the famous tripartite
division of thinking technology by means of the *respondeo dicendum*, was
adopted directly from the Catholic theology of Thomas Aquinas. Here,
the "Thomistic article"—the cubist landscape of a trinal division of
objections, respondeo, and answers to objections—allowed thought to
follow a labrynthian figure, setting objects in a dramatic tension. Which
is, of course, the core of the Baudrillardian method: a more ancient habit
of thought which follows the "S" figure of the labyrinth (Baudrillard's
descent into the degree-zero of "symbolic exchange" and the "rationalist
eschatology"). And just as McLuhan descended into the "technological
maelstrom" in order to discover therein possibilities for "epiphanies,"
for, that is, the creation of new human communities based on "aesthetic
apperception;"[22] so too, Baudrillard enters the cold universe of communication to discover therein the return of the symbolic which haunts the
terrorism of the code. McLuhan might have correctly diagnosed the
American situation as clonal of the European mind; but Baudrillard does
the opposite. He thinks technology under the sign of the mirror of
America because he diagnoses Europe as clonal of the (American) empire
of cyber-technology. Thus, McLuhan measured the empire of (American)
technology for its fatal deficiences by recuperating the classical habits of
the European mind; commenting thereby on the actual legacy of the
rationalist eschatology which, while it may have originated in the
European spirit, actually was first materialized in that curious mixture of

commerical freedom and missionary consciousness that came to be called the American lifestyle.

And Baudrillard? He is the thinker who comes late to the feast, but whose grisly readout of the virtual world of America—a reading all the more grim for the absence of the false illusions of enlightenment humanism—represents an early warning system for the future of Europe, now that it enters so quickly and without a murmur of dissent onto the path of technological liberalism. McLuhan might have *thought* power in the last dying days of rationalism, but Baudrillard theorizes Europe as the first of all the American postmoderns. Baudrillard's America, that is, as a quantum society: no history, only a virtual culture; no time, only a perfectly spatialized politics; no justice, only a contractual theory of political rights; and, finally, not even a mass society, but a society of masses, typified by the random and violent struggle of predators and parasites. Or is it just the opposite? Baudrillard's America as the recovery of real subjectivity, and of the return of myth: that world predicted by McLuhan where all the signs reverse, and the cynical turning of violence and seduction is ultimately what marks the subjectivity of the possessed individual. Which is to say that Baudrillard is the truth-sayer of McLuhan: the theorist of technology who has managed to translate McLuhan's understanding of cynical power and of virtual technology into a real materialist analysis of the mediascape. An analysis of the mediascape that has *seduction* as its language, *fractal subjectivity* as its dominant psychology, *semio-aesthetics* as the logo of its designer environ- ments, and *sub-suicidal politics* as its principle of power. A virtual world of the mediascape, that is, where mutant individuals mingle like ecoplasm in the "cold and communicational, contactual and motiva- tional obscenity of today."[23] To McLuhan's image of "vicious turtles" with their sensory organs turned inside out by electronic technologies of mass communication; Baudrillard theorizes *natural cyborgs*, drifting indifferently, actually miniature terminals, of virtual media that radiate such virulent flashes of "viral positivity" because they are already negative after-images of the death of communication. Not hysteria any longer with its theatrical staging of the autonomous subject, and certainly not paranoia with its organizational strategems of secrecy, but schizophrenia and terror.

The Theatre of Hyper-Technology

New observations by the Hubble Space Telescope have produced what astronomers say are exciting images and data on some of the most massive stars known in the universe.

The findings show two extremely large and hot stars expelling enormous amounts of matter, the apparent prelude to their ultimate demise in catastrophic explosions. Another spectacular image shows a luminous ring of matter surrounding a star that has already suffered such a fate.

New York Times, January 17, 1991

There is only technology as a theatre of seduction after Baudrillard: a universe of ambivalent signs flickering randomly between psychosis and narcosis, perfectly indeterminate in their destiny because what is at stake is the broader historical arc of a "rationalist eschatology" which, once having achieved its moment of universal triumph as the law of the code, now undergoes a violent reversal, a fantastic implosion of energy, into a catastrophic melt-down. An empire of technology, that is, which can glimmer so brilliantly because like a massive star at the moment of its death, it begins to expel "enormous amounts of matter as a prelude to its demise." A violent expulsion of the image-reservoir, a fantastic acceleration of the signs of consumption, a frenzied drive towards the technical perfectiblity of sound, images, movement, aestheticized bodies: not so much a rehearsal of a future catastrophe, but of a violent implosion of society that has already taken place. Techno-culture, therefore, as the formation of the "material rings of matter" which in their future luminosity will signal the death of the social. The theatre of hyper-technology as the violent and immensely energetic expulsion of cultural matter *after* the catastrophe. This is a universe of technology that can be so seductive because it is enfolded within this double movement of reversal: a violent centrifugal implosion of the energy of the technological dynamo, and a frenzied centripetal explosion of a dead ring of cultural matter.

Baudrillard writes eloquently about technology because he theorizes about the time after the catastrophe. Not a time of inertia, but of ceaseless movement in the eddies of cultural matter. Here, the inner logic of technology accelerates quickly beyond the realm of production (the law of value) and even beyond that of consumption (the terrorism of the code); beyond, that is, the three key orders of the law of value—the "counterfeit" logic of the classical era, the law of "production" of the industrial era, and the "simulacrum" of the cybernetic era—to a fourth order of value: the "hologramic logic" of the era of fractal capitalism. If Baudrillard can describe so well the theatre of hyper-technology in all of its mutations, from primitive productivist logic to the floating density of the hologram, it is because his theory *is* technology. In actuality, his is a hologramic text in which the experience of reading Baudrillard provides a privileged moment of entry into a deeply familiar territory: re-experiencing, that is, our own fractal subjectivity as it is blasted apart by the violent expulsion of techno-culture that illuminates the darkening horizon. And if Baudrillard's theory of hyper-technology can move so quickly, if it can reverse itself without warning, if it represents an endless play of ironic doublings, that is because Baudrillard is also caught up in the spell of an astronomical logic that he thought he was only describing. Each of Baudrillard's writings on techno-culture, which is to say *all* of his writings—from the challenge to the order of productivist value in *The Mirror of Production* and the frenzied simulacra of *In the Shadow of the Silent Majorities* and *Oublier Foucault* to the post-catastrophe theorems of *La Transparence du mal*—are part of the violent expulsion of matter spun off by technological society as it undergoes its terminal implosion of energy. Not a mournful writing either, but social texts that enter enthusiastically into the equivalence of speed and death because they are already their own luminous rings of dead matter. Baudrillard's theory of technology, then, as already a negative after-image of the burnout of his thought in the astronomical logic, the catastrophe theorems, of the social universe. Consequently, the injunction: read Baudrillard as the the first of all the social theorists of technology who burning through the four orders of the law of value, from productivist logic to the dispersion of the code into cultural fractals, floats now through the cultural scene as a brilliantly luminescent ring of dead words, dead thoughts, and dead strategems. At the epochal moment of the *fin de millennium*, might it not also be said of Baudrillard, what Nietzsche once suggested of that terrible knowledge of "cynical power,"[24] who would have the courage for that, who could faithfully follow Baudrillard's thought as it retreats *ahead of culture* into the "transparency of evil?" Who, that is, having followed Baudrillard's "fatal strategy" as it speed-reads the simulacra of technological society, could then do to Baudrillard what he has done so many times to his chosen objects of critique, from politics and sexuality to advertising? That is, read Baudrillard with the violence of a particle accelerator, forcing his thought to implode into the dark density of the nucleic energies of a black hole. And in that speed reading of Baudrillard, know that we have finally come home to the most intimate, the most intensely historical, and the most radically ideological of all theories of technology. To make of Baudrillard an epochal sign of that which has been done to us, and by us, as we arc into gleaming rings of dead techno-meat: satellites in orbit around bodies and thoughts which are now only a *mise en scène* of our fatal disappearance into the theatre of simulacra.

For that is the irony of course. Baudrillard, the theorist who, after Foucault, most deeply subverts the humanist conception of subjectivity as a dead referent, can now only be read under the sign of the challenge of the personal. Just as Camus suggested that all thought is in the way of a radical "undermining" of received truths, so too are Baudrillard's negations—of Marxism, positivism, existentialism, semiotics, and cultural materialism—in the order of a radical undermining of the intellectual horizon of "viral positivity." Baudrillard can achieve such widespread international acclaim and, equally, be the object of such bitter criticism because in his rewriting of the Western myth of the rationalist eschatology, he is the fatal truth-sayer of the ethical complicity of the contemporary horizon of thought in sustaining the law of value, from the political critics of the production machine of advanced capitalism to the theoretical strategists of radiating positivity. Baudrillard's myth-making occurs at just the point where conditions of preservation are sublimated into predicates of being. And he completes Nietzsche's *Untimely Meditations* by dissolving the privileged referent of history into the phantasm of simulation: as such, his work is constitutively historical. Not only is it a semiological history of the violent ascent of the three orders of value, but an inverted history of the present reversal of the order of value by its dissolution into the delirium of the hologram. Finally, therefore, a hyper-history which, functioning under the sign of the structural law of value, speeds up the historical referent to its moment of fatal dispersion: that moment of de-simulation where, in dislodging "the structural position of each *term*, of the subject position of each of the antagonists,"[25] the history of the entanglement of the sign and mimetic violence can be written. A Baudrillardian history, then, of fatal strategies, the reversion of the law of the code into the challenge of exterminism. And, finally, a leading thinker of a French generation that was supposedly post-ideological, Baudrillard's theory of technology is intensely contaminated with ideology. Not, however, ideology as the critique of false consciousness (although, that too, in his early theorizations of reification such as in *Le Système des objets*), but a *viral ideologist* who travels deeply into hyper-reality in order to discover therein its genetic logic of disappearance and exterminism. A theorist, therefore, of the ideology of the structural law of value, where ideology comes alive, not as the will to (false) rationality but as the will to a (true) viral invasion of the body. In this sense, Baudrillard's key political texts—*Simulations, In the Shadow of the Silent Majorities, Oublier Foucault,* and *Seduction*—are in the way of epidemiological reports on the mutation of social subjects into natural cyborgs:

> ...we must think of the media as if they were, in outer orbit, a sort of genetic code which controls the mutation of the real into the hyperreal, just as the other, micro-molecular code controls the passage of the signal from a representative sphere of meaning to the genetic sphere of the programmed signal.[26]

> For two centuries now, the uninterrupted energy of the social has come from deterritorialisation and from concentration of power in ever more unified agencies. A centralised perspective space which orientates everything inserted into it by a simple convergence along the "line of "flight" (in effect, the social, like space and time opens up a perspective towards infinity). The social can only be defined from this panoptic point of view. But let us not forget that this perspective space (in painting and architecture as in politics or the economy) is only one simulation model among others, and that it is characterised only by the fact that it gives rise to effects of truth, of objectivity, of unknown and unheard of in other models. Perhaps, even this is only a *delusion*? In which case everything has been contrived and staged in this "comedy of errors" of the social and has never had any deep significance. Ultimately, things have never functioned socially, but symbolically, magically, irrationally, etc.[27]

Behind power, or at the very heart of power and of production, there is a void which gives them a last glimmer of reality. Without that which reverses them, cancels them, and seduces them, they would never have attained reality.

Besides the real has never interested anyone. It is the locus of disenchantment par excellence, the locus of simulatiom, of accumulation against death. Nothing could be worse. It is the imaginary catastrophe standing behind them that sometimes makes reality and the truth fascinating. Do you think that power, economy, sex—all the *real's* big numbers—would have stood up one single instant without a fascination to support them which originates precisely in the inverted mirror where they are reflected and continually reversed, and where their imaginary catastrophe generates a tangible and immanent gratification?[28]

But then if Badrillard can theorize so well the resuscitational ideology of the simulacrum (like surrealism as an ironic upstaging of functionality), where power most of all continuously "restages its own death"[29] in order to recharge its flagging energies, it is because his thought performs an artistic experiment in inverting spatial perspective. Not for Baudrillard the modernist space of the panoptic nor, for that matter, the classical perspective of the Renaissance, but the foregrounding of the more labyrinthian, and forgotten, perspective of the space of seduction. The space, that is, of "enchanted simulation," the trompe l'oeil, as the secret of all appearances.

There is no nature in the *trompe-l'oeil*, nor landscapes, skies, vanishing points or natural light. Nor faces, psychology or historicity. Everything is artifact. A vertical backdrop raises objects isolated from their referential context to the status of pure signs.[30]

One senses that these objects are approaching the black hole from which, for us, reality, the real world, and normal time emerge. With this forward decentering effect, this advance towards the subject of a mirror object, it is the appearance of the double, in the guise of trivial objects, that creates the effect of seduction, the startling impression characteristic of the *trompe-l'oeil*: a tactical vertigo that recounts the subject's insane desire to obliterate his own image, and thereby vanish. For reality grips us only when we lose ourselves in it, or when it captures us as our own, hallucinated death.[31]

So then, the annihilation of "the scene and space of representation," revealing finally that the real world is but a "staged" event, "objectified in accord with the rules of perspective," and thereby undermined as a *purely perspectival principle* by the "experimental hypersimulation of the *trompe-l'oeil.*"[32] Or, as Baudrillard states in a passage from *Seduction* which surely marks the end of panoptic space with its enchanted reversal into a perspective of *appearances* which is always "projected forwards":

> ...While the Renaissance organized all space in accord with a distant vanishing point, perspective in the *trompe-l'oeil* is, in a sense, projected forward. Instead of fleeing before the panoramic sweep of the eye (the privilege of panoptic vision), the "objects" fool the eye (*"trompent l'oeil"*) by a sort of internal depth—not by causing one to believe in a world that does not exist, but by undermining the privileged position of the gaze. The eye, instead of generating a space that spreads out, is but the internal vanishing point for a convergence of objects. A different universe occupies the foreground, a universe without horizon or horizonality, like an opaque mirror placed before the eye, with nothing behind it. This is, properly speaking, the realm of appearances, where there is nothing to see, where things see you.[33]

And so, a hyper-aestheticized theory of the disappearing reality of technology that has the description of the "objects" of all the designer environments (from weather and consumerism to the war machine) as its privileged focus; but which can undermine them with uncanny insights because what is put into play is nothing less than a vision of the technological eschatology as a "semio-aesthetics." A whole world of the "enchanted simulation" of appearances which, leaving behind the perspectival closure of panoptic space, are staged as a pure surface of events, without depth but for that reason no less analogical. A "semio-aesthetics" in which the "objects" of technology are "projected forward" towards the eye as its own internal vanishing point:[34] the trompe l'oeil, therefore, no longer as an artistic experiment, but as the material spatial principle for a reality, which while it may veer between the "ecstasy of communication" and the inertia of "sub-suicidal politics" is, for that reason, no less seductive.

Technology as Seduction

Only signs without referents, empty, senseless, absurd and elliptical, absorb us.

Baudrillard, *Seduction*

What if we were to think, with Baudrillard, of technology as seduction? A cold seduction that chills the heart because it charms and entices by its promise of an imminent reversibility, by its horizon of an imminent catastrophe for the sake of which it lures us on but about which it is, of course, forbidden to speak. Not technology as a referent of power which emanates elsewhere or as reducible to the language of instrumental reason, but the name given to a certain point of fatal disappearance, a violent disintegration towards which everything plunges as its final, ecstatic destiny. Not even technology now as a "rationalist eschatology," but its opposite: a dark and implosive horizon of emptiness into which the energies of living and non-living things are drained, and for the sake of which they struggle to exist.

Technology, that is, as an object of fascination only when it is about disappearances: the disappearance of commodities into signs, history into simulation, material objects into image-reservoirs, faces with memories into the surgical world of designer aesthetics, bodies into fractal subjectivity, the spoken word into communication, and panoptic space into the enchanted simulacrum of the trompe l'oeil. And all this world of disappearances, not as the false consciousness of a real antecedent world, but as the brilliant destiny, the point of imminent reversibility, towards which the language of seduction lures us, and for the sake of which it struggles to survive. If Baudrillard can say that "seduction is stronger than power because it is a reversible and mortal process, while power wants to be irreversible like value,"[35] it is because he understands that in the enchanted world of the technological eschatology, which is to say in that of the trompe l'oeil come alive, everything wants desperately to escape the terrorism of the referent, and enter into the surface play of appearances. Here, "semio-aesthetics" is the internal vanishing point for a society "without horizon or horizonality," where objects finally "see us" as servomechanisms in the theatre of seduction.[36]

A *transactional* world, therefore, where the terrorism of the code is forced to undergo a fatal, but exhilarating, reversal. No longer the accumulation of profits under the sign of the law of production, but the excesses of the consumption machine as a desperate means of participating in the symbolic feast of an image-reservoir that always runs on empty. That point where even economy takes up the challenge of seduction as the dark and invisible horizon of *consummation*—the demand for reciprocity—reinvests the object world with the energies of symbolic exchange. And transsexuality too: a fatal sign-slide between the genders, really an amnesia on the question of the sexual referent, as the meaning of the sexual is obliterated in the cold light of the "obscenity of communication."[37]

A world of sacrificial power, then, which operates at the violent edge of hyper-rationalism and primitive myth. Power that can be so deeply fascinating because it is invested with the cynical sign of imminent reversibility. A whole technology of power functioning as the closed horizon of the social space because its real language is that of sacrificial violence. Sacrificial power has nothing to do with subjectivity, since it originates in the culture of mutant individuals. A fractal zone of subjectivity that has been crushed by its processing through the mediascape. Here, possessed individualism refers to an opaque amnesic social matter—the society of the soft masses—which is the dark liquid referent through which pass, like invisible neutrinos, all the violent impulses of the mediascape. So then, sacrificial power appears as a spectacular theatre of television psy-ops on the bionic population: an aimless alternation of victims and executioners whose single political function is to provide a negative after-image, an image-reservoir of subjectivity that we insist on calling material reality, for the operations of abuse value. For, that is, the abstract cohesion of the possessed individuals of the mediascape around the forcible expulsion of semiotically nominated victims. Sacrificial violence, therefore, operating as a vicious image-reservoir in which possessed individuals and semio-victims play out in parodic form the myth of mimesis.

A perfect reversibility, then, between all the old polarities of power, sex, economy, consciousness, and sacrifice. No longer production versus consumption, use-value versus exchange-value, sign versus commodity, victim versus executioner, but a fantastically accelerated, because so depthless, alterity among all the cynical signs. Not really a human world, but a hyper-human one: that point where subjectivity inscribes itself in the commodity first, then in the sign, and finally in the sacrificial violence immanent to seduction. And where technology also finally fulfills the ancient fable by acquiring organicity: first in the reified but dull form of the commodity, then as the object (of the consumption machine) which speaks, and lastly as the spectre of evil—the fear of bodily and social contamination—which haunts the sterile perfectibility of a will to tech-nique which knows only the maximalism of "bad infinity."

After Baudrillard, there is only technology as seduction. A theory of seduction which can be so fascinating because it moves in two opposing directions at once: a historical meditation on the frenzied struggle of the rationalist eschatology—the law of value—to escape its reversal into the depthless world of symbolic exchange; and the return of primitivism, of magic, and of appearances as the dark, ecstatic, horizon which is its inevitable destiny. No closure either, but a technological eschatology which inscribes alterity into the disappearing centre of things: a language of ambivalence, irony and reversibility that mimics the world of techno-logical experience and that, as the "missing dimension" of the social, represents its deepest genetic logic.

Baudrillard's Missing Twin Star

Baudrillard's fatal contradiction is that he has forgotten what he has so often intimated in his writings: that in astrophysics every star has its double, a twin star, like the missing dark matter of deep space, which while never seen by optical scanners displays its presence in the cold universe by the invisible pull of magnetic energy that it exerts on its visibile twin. The dark twin star of seduction, Baudrillard's central concept and his way of resolving the Sartrean riddle of unreconciled experience, is that of repulsion. Not a fatal attraction to the challenge of the game, but an imminent repulsion against the gestures of an always fatal cynicism. Not a *dédoublement* marking the return of the "necessity of lack" to the impoverished law of the code, but a silence of dissent marking the furthest frontier of the impossibile limit of experience. Seduction is inscription in the "missing dimension" of the order of value; repulsion is its exile through memory; seduction a cynical sign-slide between metaphor and metonymy; repulsion a cancellation of the sign-field; seduction is the annihilation of difference except as an indifferent rule of topological play; repulsion is a dark and missing otherness of embodied subjectivity.

To say that the domain of seduction is haunted by the dark impossible presence of repulsion is, of course, to make the broader claim that it is possible to stand aside from the gravitational pull of Nietzsche's "eternal recurrence," to rupture the horizon of value within which thought and history is enucleated. But how is this possible when the game of seduction, with its labyrinth of challenges and responses unto death, allows no other twisting of a dissenting reason? To claim repulsion as the missing twin star of seduction is also to say, then, that Baudrillard is trapped within a doubling outside his own consciousness. An imminent reversibility of seduction and repulsion where human subjectivity counterpoints the cynical power of the language of seduction. That the repulsion of dissenting reason stands in an inverse relationship to seduction, representing both its fulfillment and spectre of death, is to speak really of the reenchantment of seduction by the languages of paradox, irony and ambivalence.

The hot glimmer of seduction is the ruling language of a cold time; but the dark cold possibility of repulsion is the forgotten term for that implacable stubborn presence which we call a human being.

4

_____

THE DESPOTIC SIGN:
BARTHES'S RHETORIC OF TECHNOLOGY

If there can be such an immense revival of interest in rhetoric, if, that is, the analogical tropes of rhetorical analysis can displace the semiological language of discourse theory, it is due in no small part to the contribution of Roland Barthes in understanding rhetoric as the language of power today. Not, however, the rhetoric of speaking subjects searching for *phronesis*, but the mutation of rhetoric into an oratorical machine, within which all subjectivity is constituted and on behalf of which even mythology reverts now into a sacrificial site. Through all of his texts, from *Mythologies*, *Camera Lucida*, and *Image/Music/Text* to the *Empire of Signs*, Barthes traces out the hidden tropes of power as a rhetoric machine. If he ends his life with *Barthes by Barthes* gazing nostalgically at photographs of himself with his mother, it is also due to his realization that even the name Barthes has escaped his own subjectivity and has become an indefinite and cynical sign in the rhetoric of language games; that *Barthes by Barthes* is the autobiography of a rhetoric without a subject. And Barthes knew this, and went to his death with the realization that he was himself a condition of preservation for and a justificatory ideology of the rhetoric of technology; that the age of Barthes is now the name we give to that fateful time when myth imploded beyond the antinomies of metaphor and metonymy, becoming the empire of the cynical sign.

Consequently, read Barthes not as a semiologist or as the last of the Saussearian grammaticians, but as the theorist of technology as cynical myth, of, that is, the heating up and mutation of the logic of technique into an infinite variety of empty signs.

For there is, of course, no mythology at all in Barthes's thought, only a lament for the end of mythology, an indefinite reversal of the meaning of classical mythology as a sustaining structure of belief into a succession of persuasive rhetorics. Myth as ideology, without history. His fatal insight was to understand that the real challenge of mythology, what incited interest in its fictional unities, was precisely its imminent catastrophe, its impossibile reconciliation with the opposing poles of signifier and signified. Thus, Barthes was more a prophet of crash aesthetics, of the "split in the world," which he liked to describe as the "crossing of the syntagms of metaphor and metonymy" as the venerable logic of myth in its sacrificial phase: the playing-out, that is, of myth today as a series of ambivalent, but for that matter no less spectacular, catastrophes.[1]

Barthes's game is not a new one. It responds to a more ancient impulse of the rhetoricians, from the Island of Syracuse first, and then from the Greeks, who tried to achieve through the analogical rules of rhetoric a creative unity of unreconciled experience. Its ethic is the Aristotelian quest for *phronesis*; its politics are those of a prudential theory of liberalism; its interest focuses on the world of appearances; and its ultimate legacy is what Augustine foretold in the fifth century: of the rhetoricians "only their ashes remain." A professor of classical rhetoric first and foremost, and only later a theorist of the aesthetics of designer subjectivity, Barthes's thought has the singular merit of rehearsing once again the ancient fable of rhetoric, and of witnessing once more its expiration in the ashes of experience.

The Last Happy Thinker

But then, Barthes's time has not yet come, for his is the imagination that will haunt the third millennium. In his texts are to be found in primary colors all of the forms of subjectivity which will emerge with the empire of the sign: anachronic subjectivity, humiliated repetition, the materialist subject trapped in Nietzsche's "spider web," the pleasure of frenzied consumption. A prophet of the coming phase of purely *aestheticized* capitalism, Barthes is the weary nihilist: the first and best of all the bimoderns. The thinker, that is, of the split subject: the schizoid subject who lives in the "degree zero" between pleasure and bliss, between the end of history and the triumph of ideology.

Indeed, Barthes can fully understand the process by which power acquires organicity because his writing occupies the imaginary territory of the possessed individual. Barthes can propose that we "escape culture by retreating ahead of it" and that we leave culture "by going deeply into it" since that is exactly what he has done.[2] His writing is an immensely detailed and evocative readout of the *semiolect* of possessed individualism: between fear and bliss, a materialist subject "dissolving in the constructive secretions of its web," a subject of "encratic language."[3] Barthes has *thought* the text of power to such a point of intensity that it splits apart, revealing its imminent *doxa*. He can be the first of all the bimodern subjects, because he has theorized the psychology of the split subject, of what it is like to live as a "public sook" at the degree zero of experience: a subject of "humiliated repetition" seeking the forgetfulness of "bliss."[4] But that, of course, is not surprising since by habit of intellectual training in the classical tradition of rhetoric, Barthes's formation was always that of a doubly split subject; seduced yet repelled by the imminent reversibility of the cynical sign. Horizoned by all the signs of classical rhetoric, himself an analogical trope to a public experience of surfaces without depth, Barthes's fate recapitulates that of the more ancient practice of rhetoric: the writer of the autobiography of the weary nihilist in the age of aesthetized commodification. Just because his writings are so critical and unreflexive, so caught up in Nietzsche's "spider web" as their moment of freedom, that is their lasting value. To read Barthes is to obtain an uncensored readout of nihilism in its Buddhist phase, where all is a matter of taste. Or, as Barthes says: "The best nihilism is perhaps *masked*: in some ways *interior* to institutions, to conformist discourse, to apparent finalities."[5]

Consequently, the deep complicity of Barthes and Baudrillard. In their writings is suddenly lit up the dark horizon of an empty object world, no less seductive or menacing for its static circulation of aesthetic signs. If we are forced by Baudrillard to rethink the "world as object," or by Barthes to reflect on the "empire of signs," it remains nonetheless enigmatic for us. How can we rethink the world outside of the enucleating terms within which its rhetoric encloses us, for the challenge of technology as rhetoric is that we, too, have become conditions of preservation for the prolongation of an invasive power. If that be the case, then Barthes and Baudrillard might be thought of as *hologramic thinkers*: that dense intellectual nucleus that contains within its genetic code the hidden encryptions of the destiny of the whole. To study Barthes and Baudrillard is, then, not by way of depth but through a trompe l'oeil, where we capture the deflected surface effects. To become, that is, *gnostics* in search of the disappearing key to a future rhetoric machine, not yet fully realized. And if they can write so brilliantly of the cynical sign, it is because these are theorists who have achieved an economy of depthless surface writing as a signature of the bimodern condition. Not a literature of refusal or transgression, but of a floating equivocacy, a fatal sign slide. To enter their theoretical *imaginaires* is finally to experience from *within* the meaning of exteriorized subjectivity. Ultimately what they have achieved is a virtual theory for a virtual world: a universe in which *we* become the seductive object of the cynical sign.

But then, why not? Baudrillard rethinks the mediascape under the sign of seduction, but Barthes is one better. In the literary tradition of Italo Calvino, the first writer to achieve the extraterrestrial optic of a floating, perfectly *groundless* perspectival effect, Barthes theorizes a floating seduction: seduction lived at the degree zero of pleasure and desire. Here, pleasure is like Baudrillard's seduction, but it is never really reversed, only cancelled out in an indefinite scandal of absence.

> Desire has an epistemic dignity. Pleasure does not. It seems that (our) society refuses (and ends up ignoring) bliss to such a point that it can produce only epistemologies of the law (and of its contestation), never of its absence, or better still, of its nullity.[6]

While Baudrillard, writing under the social optic of "symbolic exchange"—the traditional French affinity for the recuperation of the "magic" and "energy" of the primitive mind—takes refuge in the fatal destiny of the law of the code; Barthes is more unrelieved. In his thought, there is no trace of the romance of a "fatal strategy" or of the recuperation of "symbolic exchange;" only the endless horizon of a split experience, of which *our* subjectivity is the alchemical principle of transmutation.

Which is to say, of course, that Barthes is the contemporary Voltaire. In an eloquent essay on Balzac's Mercadet, Barthes once noted, elliptically to be sure, that Voltaire was the "first of the happy writers."[7] A thinker at the dawn of history who could refuse history, separate intellectualism and intelligibility, and "thus countenance anti-intellectualism, he could be happy." His antithesis was Rousseau who gave the moderns the "poisoned legacy" of bad conscience: the "necessity of translating their historical situation, but not the means of doing so."

> Voltaire grounded liberalism on a contradiction. As a system of non-system, anti-intellectualism excludes and gains on both counts, constantly ricocheting between bad faith and good conscience, between a pessimism of substance and a jig of form, between a proclaimed skepticism and a terrorist doubt.[8]

Is it possible that Barthes, in forswearing history (in favor of structuralism), tragedy (in favor of the parodic play of myth), and transcendence (in favor of the immobility of the image-reservoir) is the *last* of the happy writers? Not a thinker of Rousseau's bad conscience, if by that expression we mean living the tension between transcendence and inertness, but of Nietzsche's "good conscience": the writer who sets down his chair in the middle and blinks..."that is what his smirking tells us."[9] Indeed, if Barthes could remark that "Will burns us. Power destroys us. Only knowledge calms," it is because *his* knowledge lives out the anamenesis of that contradictory space lying between a "proclaimed skepticism" and a "terrorist doubt."[10] In the end, Barthes could only be a skeptic because he was a true believer in the permanent sanctity of the trope; and he could only exercise a "terrorist doubt" because he analyzed to an awesome, and epic, state of disintegration the grounds of faith of the rhetorical imagination.

Cynical Rhetoric

Barthes's thinking at the degree zero of good and bad conscience made him an ideal candidate to explore the glittering continent of cynical rhetoric: the inversion of rhetoric into an aestheticized machinery of cynical signs. No longer is it a rhetoric of embodied speech, but the enucleation of subjectivity within a talking machine: a media speech that comes alive, assumes a "throatiness," has a certain "pulsation," even a "tissue" (myth as ideology). Here, there is no rhetoric with a speaking subject, but only the invasion of subjectivity by a cynical rhetoric. A sinister rhetoric machine that stretches across the pixel sky of the mediascape. An externalized *rhetoroscope* which has the "anachronic subject" as its historical agent, the "repeating machine" of the media as its ideological apparatus, "humiliated repetition" as its strategy of cultural domination, and mythology (dehistoricized and dematerialized) as its "ideolect."[11]

This is most explicit in *The Fashion System* where Barthes disintegrates the universe of fashion into its elementary theoretical particles. Not fashion as seduction or as the reification of taste, but something much more totalizing: fashion as a vast rewriting of the body under the double signs of signifier and signified, the *minima aesthetica* of rhetoric today. Barthes speaks of the "rhetoric machine" because the fashion system is the combinatorial sign within which we are enclosed: as *nature* (Barthes describes the four seasons of nature as corresponding to the internal marketing rhythms of the fashion season); as *pleasure* (where fashion is the *ideolect* of pleasure); as *desire* (the fashion system plays at the rough edges of pleasure and bliss); as *chemistry* (Barthes speaks of the "fluidity" of fashion, where the rhetoric of the signified mutates into the pleasure of the signified object); and as *history* (Barthes's fashion system is about myth, and the erasure of embodied history).[12]

While *The Fashion System* is often criticized, even by the later "literary" Barthes, for its rigid scientism, that is its unique strength. For this text is not about fashion at all, but about the disappearance of fashion into a system of cynical signs. Not about the *rhetoric* of fashion, but the vanishing of rhetoric (both as "persuasion" and as "speech as social power") into the combinatorial (coordinates in clothing and mathematics) of cynical rhetoric. *The Fashion System* is itself a cynical sign: occupying a curious, but privileged, space between the positivistic science of signs that it thought it was only imitating, and the disappearance of the sign into the text of the social body. In this book science as a purely fictional language, always promising a provisional coherence for experience, mutates into a system of power: a power code in the *form* of fashion that can be all the more sinister in its ideological hegemony because it occupies a zone of low epistemological visibility. Not the great order of politics, the transgressive realm of sexuality nor the discourse of moral prohibitions, but power as inscribing itself now in the previously untheorized zone of clothing: the writing of fashion. And, of course, it is not writing in the historical sense of an embodied, signatured text, cut across the grain of memory, voice and audience, but an alienated, yet no less seductive, writing without a sound. What Barthes would later come to describe as the utopia of the "rustle of language."

> Thus, it is happy machines which rustle. When the erotic machine, so often imagined and described by Sade, an "intellectual" agglomerate of bodies whose amorous sites are carefully adjusted to each other— when this machine starts up, but the convulsive movements of its participants, it trembles and rustles: in short, it *works*, and works well. Elsewhere, when today's Japanese surrender themselves en masse, in huge halls, to the slot-machine game called pachinko, these halls are filled with the enormous rustle of the little balls, and this rustling signifies that something, collectively, is working: the pleasure (enigmatic for other reasons) of playing, moving the body with exactitude. For the rustle...implies a community of bodies: in the sounds of the pleasure which is "working," no voice is raised, guides or swerves, no voice is constituted; the rustle is the very sign of plural delectation— plural but never massive (the mass, quite the contrary, has a single voice, and terribly loud).[13]

The "rustle" of a pleasure that is *working*, then, as a perfect description of the parallel play of consumers in the shopping mall: "no voice is raised, guides or swerves, no voice is constituted." Indeed, there is no voice at all, except the "rustle" of the fashion system as a "community of (isolated) bodies" which is working with exactitude the pleasure nerves of consumption.

Consequently, *The Fashion System* can be so brilliant as a hyper-positivistic description of the method (rhetoric) by which the science of signs takes possession of the body because it is politically naive. Naive, that is, about the vanishing of rhetoric into the cynical sign, the disappearance of fashion into the ideolect of the code, and the erasure of writing into a radical semiurgy. But it is precisely on account of Barthes's political innocence, and his mythic pretension to "cover the world with writing"— from photography and advertising to myth and fashion—that his work provides such a privileged glimpse of the semiurgical operations of the *law of the code*. Here to be discovered is an epistemological primer for understanding the disappearance of the body into the sign of seduction, or what is the same, into the fashion system. If like all the classical rhetoricians from the Island of Syracuse before him, Barthes could not in the end recommend a means for dynamically reconciling the fatal antinomies of experience, that does not undermine his lasting importance as the intellectual in whose imagination are rehearsed the silent codes of the horizon within which we are enclosed. Which is only to say that Barthes's formal semiotic texts, ranging from *The Fashion System* and *The Pleasure of the Text* to *Mythologies* and *Image/ Music/Text*, have a larger political importance as the basic building documents of social relativity theory. These works are to be taken seriously as a "science of signs": not however as classical Newtonian physics with its realist erasure of the sign, but as Einsteinian physics with its promise of the disappearance of the real into the fictional unity of the sign. In Barthes's writings, relativity theory ceases to be only a science of the physical universe, descending as it does into the flesh of the social universe: perfectly realistic, because it is an intensely, fictional account of our entrapment in a grammatical attitude come alive.

But then, the proto-surrealism of *The Fashion System* displays an eerie resemblance to another important rewriting of the social universe, this time the empirical domain of political experience which is dissolved into the abstract cybernetic order of David Easton's *The Political System*.[14] Both texts are exactly the same in that they are less about fashion or politics respectively, than about the vanishing of the directly experienced process of human action into an overarching systemic logic. While Barthes sought in his writing to remake the world into a system of narrative closure, Easton attempted, with exactly the same insight into power as reification, to rethink politics in the virtual language of narratology. And, of course, if there could be such a perfect complicity between the teleonomic languages ("putative necessity") of *The Fashion System* and *The Political System*, it was because both Barthes and Easton worked a common intellectual terrain: an understanding of the 'system' as the transcendental signifier of autonomous culture. While Easton was doomed in advance by an earnestly American pragmatic habit of thought to reduce the political system to a banal functionalism for its explanation (the political system as an adaptive stimulus-response model of close-circuited information), Barthes enjoyed the tremendous (European) advantage of pouring into his wide-ranging studies of dominant cultural systems—the system of myth-making(*Mythologies*), the photography system (*Camera Lucida*), the system of the image-repertoire (*Image/Music/Text*), the system of signs in ruins *(Empire of Signs)*—a sophisticated understanding of the intellectual history of structural linguistics. In a way that, for example, the American social theorist, Talcott Parsons, could only envy as he tried throughout his life to rewrite his epic book, *The Social System*, into a theory of the social as a floating sign-system. Barthes, on the other hand, imported into the datum of cultural experience a prefabricated model of the sign,[15] where the common European home-land of structural linguistics—Jakobson, Martinet, de Saussure, Hjelmslev, and Togeby—is summed up in topological relations of difference (signi-fication) and indifference (antiphrasis). This is a reified, and entirely functional, model of sign-language which, if it could be so exhaustive in the semiotic breakdown of its privileged objects (fashion as a "rhetoric of the signified"; photography as a crossing of the *studium* and *punctum*; advertising as the ideolect of Lacan's image-repertoire), it was because Barthes was the (disappearing) author of a 'theory fiction,' of a simulacrum of sensuous signs which consists, as he said in the "The Imagination of the Sign," of "intellect added to the object."[16] The inventor, that is, of a perfectly rhetorical, because deeply *persuasive*, model of signification which, not content to remain within the shadowy horizon of epistemol-ogy, insisted like a mythic Phoenix on rising from the dry ashes of the Word, and becoming a Thing. That, at least, is how Barthes introduced the "method" of *The Fashion System*, as he recounted in the most eloquent of rhetorical terms the *virtual remapping* of fashion in the reified form of two systems of information: a specifically linguistic system and a "vestimentary" system, "according to which the garment (prints, accessories, a pleated skirt, a halter top, etc.) signifies either the world (the races, springtime, maturity) or Fashion."[17] And then, Barthes notes, almost by way of afterthought the disappearance of the world from the fashion system: "These two systems are not separate: the vestimentary system seems to be overtaken by the linguistic system."[18] The world, then, rewritten in the strange language-loops of the floating sign: never pure denotation or perfect connotation, never signifier or signified, never genera or species, but a dynamic *matrix*, a Kantian "combinatorial," within which are exchanged the elementary social particles of signifying action. *The Fashion System*, therefore, as a system of "written clothing"— the way in which the transcendental order of cybernetics is inscribed in culture, with every consumer a "signifying unit."

Liquid Ideology

Barthes's description of the fashion system, with its reductive, perfectly functional logic of signification, provides an unrelieved world of language closure, that's because *it was* closed, and Barthes was not only aware of this but actually sought to intensify the understanding of the suffocating grasp of culture on social identity. Not for Barthes Baudrillard's penchant for the romanticism of primitive myth as an antidote to the terrorism of the code— the living out of the Sartrean project in ruins—nor, for that matter, the recurrence, like Foucault, to a tragically flawed conception of the aestheticized body.

Barthes was different. His thought hovered between an ideologically charged critique of the "rhetoric machine" and an unrepentant fascination with Sartre's recuperation of the gestural world of the imaginary (*The Fashion System* is dedicated to Sartre's *L'Imaginaire*). Barthes's thought was Janus-faced: an ambiguous, ironic and paradoxical mediation between the "intraworld" of ideology and the utopia of bliss (where language is clothed in flesh). Never a performative agent of ideology-critique in the Marxian sense of subordinating the question of ideology to the ritualistic actions of the commodity-form, and spurning the reading of ideology as a transparent translation of class-interests, Barthes transformed the theory of ideology by removing that concept from the realm of contestational ideas and interests to a more endrinological zone:

"libidinal technology." Barthes was the first theorist of *liquid ideology*, of a floating ideology which, taking the form of the cynical sign, refused final resolution either as pure signifier or as the condensed object of signification. In Barthes's world, ideology finally unburdens itself of the constraints of epistemology, and begins to breathe, desire, and consume. In a way remarkably similar to Althusser's theorization of language as the ideological interpellation of subjectivity, Barthes could make of ideology the liquid language of a thousand myths: the ruling myths of the "image-repertoire"— photography, fashion, popular culture, and architecture.[19] Here, the remapping of the social universe through the libidinal flows of ideology could interpellate subjectivity through its control of the *rhetorical forms* of communication. Not, however, ideological interpellation for the benefit of a final political referentiality, like Althusser's 'ideological state apparatus', but something much more ominous: the saturation of the social universe by a liquid ideology that enfolds experience within the dynamic imperatives of a technology of communication. Here, finally, ideology speaks as the truth of power that constitutes itself as a cynical sign, and traverses the social scene as a semiological war machine.

No longer power under the sign of blood nor of the disciplinary code, but power in its terminal phase as an immense technological impulse towards aestheticization. A power that speaks with the fluidity of an oratorical machine: a rhetorical power which can be so ideogrammatic because it takes possession of the tropes of fashion, music, advertising, and, most of all, subjectivity. This is a power that functions as an oratory machine, in which there is no speaking subject because the machinery of rhetoric now issues from the deepest sinews of culture and society. Hence, a power that operates as a seductive, but also forbidding, order of signs emerges as the challenge of the signs of rhetoric which install themselves in our desires (the rhetoric of sexuality), scopophiliac pleasures (the rhetoric of fashion), auditory imagination (the rhetoric of music), politics (the rhetoric of managed politics), and imaginary dream-states (the rhetoric of cinema, video and TV). A libidinal machinery of rhetoric which moving at the violent edge of synchrony and diachrony, of metaphor and metonymy, crosses all the sign-forms, only to cancel *us* finally in the equation of a ceaseless oration without a speaker, a rhetoric without a subject.

For this is one oratorical machine that no one controls, but which for that very reason deploys its logic as the constitutive ground of all other forms of power— sexuality, economy, politics, the unconscious. A rhetoric that must always remain without origin since to discover its generative beginnings would be to extinguish its cynicism. And rhetoric must always be cynical, free to float as the sliding ground at the degree zero of history and intelligibility, since a cynical rhetoric is its only possible condition of public acceptability. A cynical rhetoric, that is, which is always a sign of that which never existed: the spiraling movement *en abyme* endlessly transforming the combinatorial of power.

Barthes is explicit about the primacy of the rhetoric machine as the locus of ideology and power today. Thus, for example, in the emblematic analysis of liquid ideology, *The Pleasure of the Text*, Barthes analyses power as a rhetoric machine, performing according to three lexical rules:

First, the rule of the "repeating machine" where "encratic language" (the language proscribed by official power) is necessarily a language of ceaseless repetition. For Barthes, all institutions of official culture share a common destiny as repeating machines: "schools, sports, advertising, popular songs, news, all continually repeat the same structure, the same meaning, often the same words: the stereotype is a political fact, the major figure of ideology."[20] Here, Barthes's analysis of the encrustation of ideology in repeating images, repeating words, repeating news—a whole repeating mediascape—parallels the earlier analysis of the Frankfurt critical theorists (Adorno, Horkheimer, Brunswick) in *The Authoritarian Personality* where they, too, reported in their cultural critique of the origins of fascism in America that stereotypy and projection are the ruling psychological formulae for the creation of the authoritarian character-type. But while the Frankfurt theorists traced the origins of stereotypy to the psychological distress of the bourgeois ego under the twin pressures of an outer and inner anxiety, Barthes went one step further. Recalling Nietzsche's aphorism that "truth" is only the "solidification of old metaphors," Barthes spoke of stereotypy as a fantastic piling-up of the residues of a dead culture, with such velocity that these dark after-images of the death of the social suddenly condense into the ruling canons of the image-repertoire. The stereotype can be the "present path of truth...the feature which shifts the invented ornament to the canonical, constraining form of the signified"[21] because it is the repetition of the "official form." For Barthes, ideology in the culture of signification is always about the control of the degree zero: those multiple fractured translation points of metaphor and metonymy, which spiral across the glimmering nebula of the mediascape.

Second, the rule of "humiliated repetition," where "content, ideological schema, the blurring of contradictions —these are repeated, but the superficial forms are varied: always new books, new programs, news items, but always the same meaning."[22] And why not? For Barthes, "myth is depoliticized speech": that point where bourgeois ideology flees the world of politics, and sinks into the tissue of everyday life. If Barthes can claim that the bourgeoisie is the first class that seeks its (semiological) disappearance *as a class,* it is because it renounces history in favor of mythology. A bourgeois class acquires hegemony, because its interests coincide perfectly with the coming to be of the fully realized technological state and because in saturating the social universe with the rhetoric of mythology it sublimates its interests in the deepest *forms* of seduction. Always, then, the proliferation of new mythologies across the mediascape in direct proportion to the solidification of the second(symbolic) and third (syntagmatic) order chains of bourgeois signifiers in culture and society.

Third, is the rule of political illusion as the basis of petit-bourgeois culture.

> No significance (or bliss) can occur, I am convinced, in a mass culture (to be distinguished, like fire from water, from the culture of the masses), for the model of this culture is petit-bourgeois. It is characteristic of our (historical) contradiction that significance (bliss) has taken refuge in an excessive alternative: either in a mandarin *praxis*...or in a utopian idea (the idea of a future culture, resulting from a *radical, unheard-of unpredictable* revolution, about which anyone writing today knows only one thing: that, like Moses, he will not cross over into it.[23]

Here, Barthes approaches Baudrillard's reading of the social as revolving around that "spongy referent, that opaque but equally translucent reality, that nothingness: the masses."[24] But whereas Baudrillard begins with the inertia of the masses as the imaginary representation of the death of the social, Barthes recuperates the utopian possibility of language itself as the beckoning horizon, the moment of bliss, beyond the seamless web of mythology. Just because he has thought so deeply the suffocating immensity of "encratic language," he has also recognized in the cultural texts of bourgeois mythology the memory of another language, another *tissue*, which opposes an anachronic bliss against the pleasure of the text. Not the text as a tissue "behind which lies, more or less hidden, meaning (truth)," but the "generative idea that the text is made, is worked out in perpetual interweaving":

> lost in this tissue—this texture—the subject unmakes himself, like a spider, dissolving in the constructive secretions of its web. Were we fond of neologisms, we might define the theory of the text as an *hyphology* (hypos is the tissue and the spider's web).[25]

Barthes is, therefore, the theorist as *hyphologist*: the thinker who recurs to language as a way of finally overcoming the closed horizon of Nietzsche's spider web: that is, Nietzsche's warning in *The Will to Power* that the distinguishing feature of contemporary nihilism would be a double closure of the horizon. Not only the closure of the contents of nihilism (Barthes's "mythology as depoliticized speech"), but, of more importance, the troubling paradox that in the age of a cynical power which constitutes the horizon within which we live, we can never be certain that the questions posed, the demands for meaning uttered against the silence of the universe, are not themselves the fatal stratagems of a power, which having no basis in referential finalities, requires for its sustenance the subject who unmakes himself, actually dissolves "in the constructive secretions of (the spider's) web." Here, language, most of all, is Nietzsche's spider web: the closing of the horizon within the *topos* of a rhetoric machine which can speak the double text of metaphor and metonymy so well because language itself is *tissue* without blood, without ground.

But if Barthes's critique of the depoliticized orbit of the masses is itself a condition of preservation for cynical mythology, it is not to deny the ideological acuity of his political theory. While other theorists of contemporary ideology could rise sociologically to discuss the relationship of ideology and domination (Giddens), ideology as "glassy background" to technology (Habermas), ideology as discourse (Lefort), or ideology as a political "apparatus" of domination (Althusser), none surpassed Barthes as a diagnostician of the ways in which ideology as mythology—wrestling, the *Tour de France*, toys, ornamental cookery—

sinks beneath the surface of bourgeois society, taking possession of subjectivity in the manner of a "huge internal parsite."[26]

Thus, for example, *Mythologies* is one of the few existent texts on ideology which seeks to understand culture by going into it as deeply as possible. It is the degree-zero of ideology: the moment when Barthes's mind is simultaneously adrift in the pleasure of mythology and distanced from its process of translation of a "semiological system into a factual one."[27] Here, the horizon of everyday social life is spread out in the form of a series of meditations on myth, which, like cuts in the text, study the semiological sign-slide at the disappearing centre of things: the "jet-man" as half-flesh/half robot; the seduction of Einstein's calculation of $E = mc^2$ as rooted in the challenge of gnosticism; the triumph of plastics as the emergence of a new philosophy of nature—artificial Matter— with its abolition of the hierarchy of Substances; "soap-powders and detergents" as mythologies of the liberation of the object from its "circumstantial imperfection."[28] It is a deeply "factual" book which, like *The Eiffel Tower* after it, can investigate so closely the social microphysics of cultural experience, because this is not a text about mythology at all, but about the vanishing of language, and classical myth too, into ideology.[29] At least that is what Barthes claims in the brilliant concluding chapter of *Mythologies*—"Myth Today"—where he enumerates the specific semiological strategies of bourgeois ideology.

A study of the semiotics of the mediascape results which has few rivals in terms of its historical specificity and ideological rigor. A sweeping vision of the disappearance of history into myth ("myth gives in return a *natural* image of this reality"),[30] of the "statistical association" of myth with the right, and of the abolition of social contradictions in favor of a blissful vision of the "simplicity of essences." Barthes's object of study is a world without depth, only surfaces; a culture without dialectics, no internal mechanism of change—only the *camera lucida* of appearances. It is a society without the traces of speech—only the metalanguage of mythology. A *rhetoric* of bourgeois myth that is involved in a more fundamental struggle between history and absence: the dream-state of an "ex-nominating process" by a social class (the bourgeoisie) "which does not want to be named."[31]

What began with Marx's epic description of the "alienation" of the commodity-form, continued with Weber and Lukàcs's theorizations of "reification," and was transformed by Baudrillard's "simulation" as the model of symbolic exchange under the sign of consumption, has its culmination in Barthes's "mythology." No longer mythology as a great rupture in the tradition of critical thought, representing a semiological effacement of the history of the concept of alienation—from the originary (Marxian) concept of alienation to reification and, thereupon, to simulation; but mythology as a fantastic condensation of alienation into a dark, dense state of ideological congealment. That point where myth eats history, where metaphor enfolds metonymy, and where mythology is so intensely political that it mutates into "depoliticized speech" for depoliticized masses. Mythology as political violence to such a point of extremity, and popular invisibility, that it can be spoken of as the age of the "end of ideology."

This is only to say that on the question of ideology and domination, Barthes is a viral theorist. No longer theory which speaks as the sovereign subject from the outside, but Barthesian theory as a viral agent that works according to three biological rules: invasion of the host (the actual studies of *Mythologies*); cloning of its master genetic code (the rhetoric machine); and the replication of the virus using the dying energies of the organism ("mythology as depoliticized speech").[32] And not just parasitical, but a viral theory that works to speed up the deep logic of the genetic code in order for the host organism (bourgeois culture) to be compelled to disclose its secret. Consequently, Barthes's *utopia*—playing at the edge of pleasure and bliss—as the end of a hyper-politics of invasion, cloning and instantaneous replication.

Because Barthes is a viral theorist, adopting an endrocrinological attitude towards ideology, he can understand so well the genetic logic (rhetoric) of bourgeois society. Thus, in the famous chapter, "Myth Today," Barthes approaches the text of mythology as a living tissue, involved in the dissolution of subjectivity into a "coaenaesthesis of motionless."[33] The rhetorical strategies employed are those of "sacrificial history:" rendering the actual material process of historical struggle—the object itself—mute and immobile by the mythification of individual and collective consciousness. A vision of informational culture, therefore, as a site of Hobbesian images: cultural life as an empty field of cynical power—pervaded by fear, and requiring, for its resolution, the alienation of individual powers to the leviathan of the image-repertoire. An image-repertoire thus consisting, like the radiating debris from the big bang of an already dead universe, of the alienation of human subjectivity. Images encrusted with the loss of human memory and embodied subjectivity, which, if they can be so dazzling in their mythic appeal, it is probably because they are already brilliant afterimages of the implosion of history. Sacrificial images which embody in their *rhetorical form* the disappearance of culture and society into the virtual world of the cynical sign.

"Myth as depoliticized speech," therefore, as a vision of informational culture as a set of medical procedures by which bourgeois "pseudophysis" is traumatized by an apparatus of violent rhetorical procedures: the *innoculation* of culture with a brief privileged glimpse of the "little accidental evil" of a class-bound institution so as to immunize its understanding of the "principal evil"; the application of strategies of deterritorialization and decontextualization in order to deprive history of any specificity (in myth, "history evaporates"); the psychological strategy of *identification* by which the "Other" within the petit-bourgeois mind is externalized, then scapegoated; *tautology*—"the saving aphasia"—in which there is a double murder: "one kills rationality because it resists one; one kills language because it betrays one;" and the *statement of fact* ("myths tend towards proverbs") by which bourgeois aphorisms are projected outwards, like universal maxims: a "second-order language which bears on objects already prepared."[34] Never really the death of history, but the opposite: a parasitical relationship between myth and history, in which myth simultaneously drains the living energy of history (its embodying host), while never finally exterminating it.

Or, as Barthes states:

> For the very end of myths is to immobilize the world: they must suggest and mimic a universal order which has fixated once and for all a hierarchy of possessions. Thus, every day and everywhere, man is stopped by myths, referred by them to this motionless prototype which lives in his place, stifles them in the manner of a huge internal parasite and assigns to his activity the narrow limits within which he is allowed to suffer without upsetting the world.[35]

What Nietzsche once noted in *The Will to Power* about the coming sublimation of "becoming" by the "will to will" of a nihilistic power thus finds its final validation in Barthes's writing of the "Zodiacal signs of the bourgeois universe: the Essences and the Scales." Here, bourgeois ideology mutates history into *"essential types,"* like the "cuttlefish which squirts its ink in order to protect itself," immobilizing, fixating, cataloguing and purifying the world. And the Scales? That is, of course, the subjectivity of the possessed individual: "bourgeois morality will essentially be a weighing operation, the essences will be placed in scales of which bourgeois man will remain the motionless beam."[36]

The Alchemy of Technology

When speaking of the relationship between art and technology, Marshall McLuhan once suggested the image of art as a *probe* which serves as an early warning system of coming transformations in technological society. In Barthes's image-repertoire, it is exactly the opposite: not art as an metaphor for key transformations in the field of technological change, but technology as a critical probe of coming transitions in the field of art. Technology, that is, as the most intensive expression possible of what art, both as creative activity and institutional network, has always aspired to, but never achieved—the full aestheticization of experience. Perhaps that is why Barthes's *Mythologies* can achieve such an economy of brilliance: they are minimalist artistic tableaus, exploding with the density of the sign. And so, a maximalist technology of liquid signs (*Empire of Signs*), a high performance phase of technological production with the body as an artistic servomechanism ("The Jet Man"), crash aesthetics (*Image/Music/Text*), and even a situationist technology ("The Eiffel Tower" as the mirror of the doubled sign).[37]

Indeed, there is a visual artist, Tony Tascona, whose method of understanding technology is remarkably similar to Barthes's. An artist of transmutations, Tascona's imagination privileges those invisible chemical transitions, the chaotic gradient of chemical break-points, at which things abruptly alter states. Thus, for example, explaining his fascination with the fluid world of resins, Tascona says: "I like to see things happen, how they actually evolve and crystallize." Not just a detached student of chemical transformations either, Tascona makes of his own body an experimental site: "I like to go out in the winter sunlight, to see what will happen...I like transitions."

Barthes's theoretical imagination is like that. He makes of his body and mind an experimental site for understanding technology. Equally, he privileges chemical transitions, those fluid changes of state at which objects suddenly mutate and shift fields. Thus, in his wonderful book on photography, *Camera Lucida*, he recurs time and again to photography as "radiant emanations;" and in his essay on "Plastic," he speaks of "miracles."[38] We might say that Barthes is less a structuralist or a thinker engaged in an empirio-criticism of the sign, than an artist studying intently the liquid flow of the image-repertoire as it abruptly alters state: from signifier to signified, from metaphor to metonmy, from pleasure to bliss. He is, above all, a chemist of the cynical sign. In the same way that Tascona makes of himself a "public sook" in the winter sun, Barthes makes of his writing a deep immersion in the techological language of the liquid sign. A liquid structuralist, he focuses on language because this is the altered state in which technology is most intensively experienced in the age of teleonomic logic.

To say this, though, is only to note that Barthes revives a more classical habit of mind: alchemy. If Barthes's structure of thought privileges not finalities, but metamorphosis, mutation and sudden transitions, it is because his theory of mythology is cast in medievalist terms. It was Barthes's privileged insight to understand that the rhetoric of technology is not about things, but about the "anxious object," that is, about the transition of objects from one state to another. And so, he breathes the language of medievalism into a strikingly postmodern theory of technology, where the universe is perfectly aestheticized, and only the empire of sensuous signs continues to exist. In doing so, a magical insight appears. That the rhetoric of technology is really about a fantastic inversion, where technique carries into the contemporary century under the banner of "pleasure"—the epistemic ideology of myth—more occult medievalist practices: alchemy, gnosticism, theosophy. A more primitive fascination with altered states underlies the seduction of the cynical sign. This can only mean, however, that the empire of signs accelerates towards the medieval age.

But then, why not? In his essay, "The Structuralist Activity" Barthes described structuralism as the activity of creatively reconstructing the object. A *mantic* activity, following in the Greek tradition of mimesis, which "like the ancient soothsayer..speaks the locus of meaning but does not name it."[39] Because literature is a mantic activity

...it is both intelligible and interrogating, speaking and silent, engaged in the world by the courage of meaning which it remakes with the world, but disengaged from the contingent meanings which the world elaborates: an answer to the man who consumes it yet always a question to nature, an answer which questions and a question which answers.[40]

A chemist of the liquid sign—a thinker who dared to think language as technology at its degree-zero—it was Barthes's fate to be that dynamic transitional point where, in his own words, "the simulacrum is intellect added to the object."[41] Barthes, then, as an alchemist of technology: in whose imagination of the sign structuralism returns to history, relinking the material with the ideological, form with expression; and all this in an "empire of signs" that is ceaselessly mutating from the symbolic to the systematic and, thereupon, to the syntagmatic.

The Decay of Memory

Perhaps Barthes's mind is purely architectural: a "violent edge" which actively seeks to evoke turbulence by out-mythifying mythology, by cross-circuiting all of the key signifiers of contemporary culture. Has theory as a pure architectural gesture ever been attempted? I think not, except in the artistic imagination of Salvador Dali, and specifically in two of his paintings: *The Persistence of Memory* and the *Disintegration of the Persistence of Memory*. In a prophetic reprise of the violent edge of Barthes's thought, the tragic antinomies of technological experience are rehearsed. *The Persistence of Memory*, a creation of Dali's imagination before the Holocaust of World War II, is a paradisical painting. Here, time is fluid, amorphous and lush: a fleshy time which holds memory and possibility in the balance, and where the human imagination is itself the crucible of choice. An eco-time where the correlations of memory, creativity and situation make for the beginning of a new "otherness"—a horizon beyond the event—and the termination of the dead time of scientific mechanism. But, of course, it is just the opposite with the *Disintegration of the Persistence of Memory*, which is not about memory at all, but about the triumph of a cynical spatializing power: where the tentative and fragile horizon of a memoried time is suppressed from view. Not fluid time, but the disappearance of time into the mechanized exterminisms of contemporary European culture: time without memory, creativity, or horizon. The death of time, that is, as the epithet of the body.

The tension between these two Dali paintings captures evocatively and brilliantly Barthes's own knowledge of culture in ruins. Here, Dali is a precursor of the Barthesian imagination: a theorist who etched in words what Dali had earlier painted in colors and forms—the terminal break-down of life itself within the dead apparatus of the mediascape.

Indeed, to read Barthes's last books, from *Barthes by Barthes* to the *Empire of Signs*, is to enter into the dark fatal side of the famous science of signs which Barthes theorized. Here, the apparatus of the sign becomes hegemonic, the transcendental signifier of a culture which has assumed a species-like existence. It becomes an empire of signs that is simultane-ously about the indefinite proliferation of a viral culture, and about the silenced territory of the *absences* which mark the erasures of the sign. A world defined by photography as a constructed image-repertoire, but where photography cancels out embodied memory. A society marked by the signature of an infinite acceleration of the apparatus of mythology, but where myth itself—the relationship of voice, memory, and place—is banished. A mediascape that works ceaselessly the three primary chains of signification—the symbolic, systematic and syntagmatic—but which itself functions to exterminate questions of ethical significance. A machinery of rhetoric that is distinguished by the explosion of the primacy of language into *the* discourse of power, but which acts just as assiduously to disappear individual speech, to vaporize, that is, speech as the coincident site of history, body, and utterance. The whole science of semiology, which is about the disintegration to excess of the originary, mythic act of the sign serves as a symbolic reminder of the relationship between synchrony and diachrony, between the intimations of mythol-ogy and the projections of the historical imagination.

If Barthes's life ended with a melancholy foreboding of the *inutile* of the structuralist project, and with a desperate attempt to recover the fragments of the poetic imagination as a barrier against the *sturm und drang* of the cynical sign, it was not that he was unaware of his coming fate. At the conclusion of his essay on "The Structuralist Activity," Barthes had this to say about structuralism as a mediation of the material and the intelligible, the ideological and the aesthetic:

...precisely because all thought about the historically intelligible is also a participation in that intelligibility, structuralist man is scarcely concerned to last; he knows that structuralism, too, is a certain form of the world, which will change with the world; and just as he experiences his validity (but not his truth) in his power to speak the old language of the world in a new way, so he knows that it will suffice that a new language of history, a new language which speaks *him* in turn, for his task to be done.[42]

Barthes's ultimate fate, though, is more prosaic. The legacy of a moment in the longer gesture of language as it rewrites the world is not for him, rather the erasure of language, and of the memory of the "structuralist" Barthes with it, in an image-repertoire that crushes the memory traces of language. And not a "new language of history" either, but an image-repertoire which compresses history to that moment of fatal density where it suddenly mutates into its opposite sign-form: the graviton of anti-history, and of anti-language and anti-memory. That indefinable, purely structuralist, point where Barthes, the ancient soothsayer of history, disappears; and we are left with his brilliant residue trapped in image-simulacrum of culture. The fading image of Barthes, that is, completing the fable of rhetoric by becoming that which he thought he was only describing from afar. Indeed, might not it be said of the image-residue of Barthes what Octavio Paz once wrote about de Sade:

You have not disappeared.
The letters of your name are still a scar
that will not heal,
the tattoo of disgrace on certain faces.

Prisoner in your castle of crystal of rock
you pass through dungeons, chambers and galleries,
enormous courtyards where the still black poplars dance.
 All is mirror!
Your image persecutes you.

Man is inhabited by silence and by space.
How can this hunger be met and satisfied?
How can you still the silence? How can the void be
peopled?
How can my image ever be escaped?

Octavio Paz, *The Prisoner*[43]

5

Becoming Virtual (Technology):
The Confessions of Deleuze and Guattari

Boy without a Sex

Deleuze and Guattari began their most famous book, *Anti-Oedipus: Capitalism and Schizophrenia* with Richard Lindner's painting entitled *Boy with Machine.*[1]

Just perfect. A desexualized boy with a deterritorialized machine. A decoded flow of signs marking a convergence now of the social machine and the technical machine. A painterly image situated at the very beginning of this writing of the social body under the libidinal impact of the "civilized capitalist machine" as if to indicate an interpretive key for

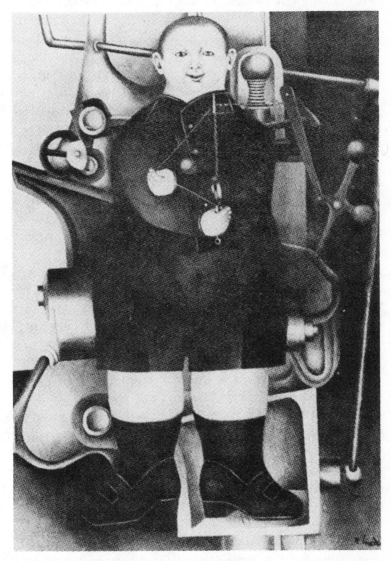

Boy with Machine, Richard Lindner (1954, oil on canvas, 40″ × 30″, Drs. Rosier and Lefer, M.D., P.A. Pension Trust)

the regime of signs to follow. Not corporeality, but the "body without organs." Not the dualism of social and non-social nature, but the quick mutation of the social machine and the technical machine into a new aesthetic synthesis. Not machinic technology, but the machine oedipalized by the boy's imagination; and not the boy as an automaton of the machine but energized by the recodings of his memories, fantasies, and understanding.

In fact, a perfect Kantian painting that sums up in a single image the synthesis of understanding (technical), imagination (synthetic) and judgment ("doubling"), which is what Deleuze and Guattari's work is all about— signification and subjectification—and against which it brings a Nietzschean scream.[2] Not a chasm between technology and boy but their already accomplished positioning as a regime of signs involving signification and subjectification. The painting, then, is not a representation, but an already experienced flow of codes that expresses on the outside what we have become on the inside. Like a mask that can be taken off to reveal the transparency of our entrapment and emancipation in a great flow of decoded signs.

There is no perspective either, but a perspectival simulacra. The foot, for example, does not stand on anything, the body swells as it moves from the head to the feet, the legs are gigantic. A perfect image, then, of "the schizoid not the signifier."[3] Or, as Deleuze and Guattari state in *A Thousand Plateaus*: "The face is absolute deterritorialization... (it) removes the head from the stratum of the organism and connects it to other strata."[4] Consequently, not the great antinomies of signification and subjectification or the "paranoic" and the "schizoid flow" as representative of a fatal division in experience, but as mirrored signs trapped in the very same logic of experience. For, after all, have we not been this way before? *Boy with Machine* is the flip side of Magritte's *Ceci n'est pas une pipe* of which Foucault wrote laconically, but accurately, that in the age of the hypermodern the real and the fake prove only the impossibility of transgression. For what is the real but an absent text of floating signs, for which the forgery can be so desperately required as a deceptive sign of its missing authenticity. And so too, with *Boy with Machine*. There is no boy here, only a floating image of oedipalized signs without a context. And no machine either, only a perspectival simulacra which, if it can allude to the presence of a machine behind the boy, only works to hide a double lie in the painting. First, that the boy is the terminus ad quem of a fantastic constellation of repression, a machinic boy, which sums up in its image the triumphant psychoanalytical slogan of Mommy-Daddy-Me, so necessary to kick-start the age of industrialization. Second, that the machine is the objectification of a more juvenile boyhood fantasy—the dream of omnipotence, of power without a body, of serial reproduction without end. Or is it the opposite? The boy as a concretization of the machine made human: the mutant form that subjectivity takes in the era of *Anti-Oedipus?* And the machine as all about the disappearance of the human into a great regime of paranoic signs?

A painting, therefore, which can be so fascinating because it is so deeply schizoid: an "event scene" which is both breakthrough and breakdown. A boy without sex, just because here the reproductive functions have already fled the body and invested the regime of machines with the always hidden male desire of an infinite circulation of all the signs of reproduction.

White Walls/Black Holes

> This is because the two groups (the schiz and the paranoic) are like determinism and freedom in Kant's philosophy: they indeed have the same "object"— and social production is never anything more than desiring-production and vice-versa—but they don't share the same law, the same regime.
>
> Deleuze and Guattari, *Anti-Oedipus*

Machines everywhere. Desiring-machines, production-machines, abstract machines of faciality, organ-machines, energy-source machines. A fantastic density of machinic values that traverses the social field, and within which subjectivity most of all enters into a theatre of death: decoded of its memories, deterritorialized of its means of reproduction, and decontextualized. The famous "body without organs"[5] as the first citizen of the state of despotic capitalism. Indeed, Deleuze and Guattari are not writers of technology. Their theory *is* a technology machine: writing without a body, for a theory machine where thought is brought under the regulatory sign of the "axiomatic." Brains too are decoded, vision decontextualized, philosophy without a tradition for machinic bodies without organs.[6] A sacrificial scene, therefore, where Deleuze and Guattari do what is most difficult: they translate writing into a degree zero point of implosion between signification and subjectification, between the social machine and the production machine. To enter the body of their texts is to initiate a fantastic psychological curvature of the dematerialization and decontexualization of one's own missing body: that labrynthian point where we can no longer be certain that the mirrored images of paranoic investment and schizophrenic irruptions, of the "white walls" of signification and the "black holes" of subjectification, are not the receding horizon of our own bleak destiny.[7] For in the great western confessional tradition, from the *Confessions of St. Augustine* to the confessional subject of Rousseau, Deleuze and Guattari have also enacted in their writing an epochal confession for the age of the hypermodern: the confessional statement of "bodies without organs." Here, the social machinery of desiring-production, having completed its consummatory feast, finally speaks. Not in an ordinary language but in the schiz language of a strange new world where images heat up and suddenly red-shift, where faces take flight from their heads, where the "smooth space" of the primitive nomads of the future clashes with the "striated space" of despotic capitalism, and where time-binding technologies rebel against the reterritorializing codes of "space-binding" technologies. This is the confession of all the humanoids, of beings half-flesh/half-metal, who, speaking from *within* the closed, liquid textuality of technology, ruminate longingly, and romantically, on a past in their telematic future.

How could it be otherwise? In the brilliant theoretical confession of Deleuze and Guattari, the more epochal struggle of Nietzsche and Kant during the fading days of the nineteenth-century finally escapes the theatre of philosophical representation, becoming the fateful "regime of signs" within which everyday life of the twentieth-century is experienced. Their great confession, the twin texts of *Anti-Oedipus* and *A Thousand Plateaus*, is a historical record of the inscription of the Kantian code— the demonic language of "predicates of existence"—onto the materiality of the social field. Here, everything is a "predicate of existence": no dialectic but the terrible simultaneity of "white walls/black holes"; a matter of "synthetic apperception" taking the materialist form of three syntheses of *Anti-Oedipus*: the "connective synthesis of production" (understanding), the "disjunctive synthesis of recording" (imagination), and the "conjunctive synthesis of consumption-consummation (reason).[8]

Why should it be otherwise since it is Kant who understood best of all that the fatal division in modern experience—signification and subjectification—could only be resolved by mutating the "predicates of existence" into "conditions of preservation": into, that is, the suppression of subjective signifiers and signified subjectivity by the decoded flows of reason. Which is to say that Kant's "predicates of existence," are Deleuze and Guattari's "decoded flows"—what they describe so poetically as the gestural "markings" investing the body by desiring-production.[9] Thus, for example, in *Anti-Oedipus* the three Kantian critiques, the Critiques of Pure Reason, Practical Reason, and Judgement, are materialized at the level of production, recording, and consumption. And if in *Mille Plateau*, there could be a fateful doubling of "signification" and "subjectification" it is another way of coding "understanding" and the "imagination" with decoded reason as the immanent principle of doubling.

Deleuze and Guattari's lasting contribution, therefore, is to have written a Kantian history of technological society—a theory of technological liberalism populated by "bodies without organs," synthesized aesthetically by the changing tastes of the "abstract machine of faciality," of musicality, of images, where there is no *ding an sich*, but the reduction of capitalism to the materialism of "axiomatic capitalism"—a mathematical operation.[10] There is a ceaseless transformation of the "predicates of existence," the deterritorialization and reterritorialization of codes, into autonomous conditions of social transformation.

If it be objected that *Anti-Oedipus* is really about the repressive agency of psychoanalysis, a political refusal of the tyranny of Oedipus, then it must also be said that this is also a "schizoanalysis" of the fateful vectoring of the consumption and desiring machines. And even this conjunction is a rewriting of the texts of Marx and Freud under the sign of the Kantian regulatory code: that is, the harmonization of production and desire as the end-point of the three "anti-oedipal" critiques.

And not uncritical texts, but just the opposite. Deleuze and Guattari are the world's first systematic theorists of technological fascism. Foucault was correct only in part, when he said of Deleuze and Guattari that they had written an ethics of resistance.[11] For this is not just an ethics of resistance, but something more indefinable and valuable: a howling scream cut across the "white wall" of signification and through the "black hole" of dead subjectivity. In their theory-machine, the fateful encounter of Kant and Nietzsche in the nineteenth-century explodes across the social field in an indefinite series of reterritorializations. Not oedipalization as a psychic struggle between Mommy-Daddy-Me, but the return of Nietzsche's "ascetic priest" to alter the direction of *ressentiment*. Not commodification, but the "decoded flows" of cynical power. Not corporeality, but "bodies without organs." Not heads, but "abstract machines of faciality." Not panoptic space, but perspectival simulacra. Not rhetoric, but the axiomatic regime of "Order-Words" as the basis of the rhetoric-machine. And not the theatre of representational power, but a cynical and fully relational power that functions in the liquid language of "networking."

In this confession, the dark shadow of Nietzsche is everywhere. Indeed, if *Anti-Oedipus* could speak so eloquently of *On the Genealogy of Morals* as the classic "ethnology" of schizoanalysis, it is because Deleuze and Guattari have thought deeply about Nietzsche's cruel description of the "debt-creditor" relationship as the basis of the despotic state, and about oedipalization explained in the more dramatic sacrificial terms of the ascetic priest and revenge-seeking subjectivity.[12] If later in *A Thousand Plateaus*, they could trace out a more subterranean tradition of "rhizomatic" resistance, from Spinoza to Artaud and Blanchot, it is only because they seek to materialize the dark, often unread, side of *The Will to Power*: that "dancing" side where Nietzsche anticipates Heidegger by speaking of 'becoming' as the horizon of the recuperated life. *Anti-Oedipus* and *A Thousand Plateaus*, therefore, as an awesome, highly parodic, political encounter between the dematerialized reason of Kant and the ethics of impossiblity of Nietzsche. Here, the political reality may be the seizure of the social world by the technical materialization of the Kantian Critiques in all of their axiomatic fury—from the possession of the face as a colonialized history of signification to the possession of the bodily organs by the consuming-machine. But it is within this terrible terrain of decoded flows, dematerialized bodies, and decontextualized desire that the image of Nietzsche suddenly appears: first as the truth-sayer of the nihilism that is oedipalization, and then as the beckoning gesture to the *arborescent* of "becoming-human," "becoming-molar," "becoming-animal."[13]

Confessions in Ruins

Of course, the real seduction of all confessions is the possibility of their imminent reversibility, their labrynthian twisting into a degree-zero zone of sacrificial violence.

The confession of Deleuze and Guattari is no exception. *Anti-Oedipus* ends on a romantic, but ultimately suffocating, note: Deleuze and Guattari's politics as the irruption of a long repressed "desire," which is the impossible "Other" haunting the capitalist axiomatic.

But is this unregulated "desire," this breakdown of the capitalist axiomatic, not exactly what "despotic capitalism" always wanted the most, but could never attain? Maybe the capitalist machine never really wanted to be confined to the sign of the Kantian code—axiomatic regulation and psychoanalytical repression—but always desperately desired a breakthrough to its cynical side—of "schizzes," of great uncoded flows of desire, the world of Anti-Oedipus. Crash capitalism. Not freedom versus determinism in the Kantian schemata, but *Crash Kant* too.[14] A liquid Kant where all the big signifiers—reason, imagination, judgement—flow together, disrupting the capitalist axiomatic. Not the old regime of capitalist signs under the ruling axiomatic of the "either/or," but a more ambivalent world of the "both/and": paranoic reactionary investments and schizoid irruptions, breakdowns and breakthroughs.

This is exactly what is accomplished in *A Thousand Plateaus*, supposedly the logical culmination of *Anti-Oedipus*, but actually its scene of sacrificial collapse and dissolution. Here, the repressed differences in the great regime of signs—paranoic investment versus schizoid irruptions, decoding versus coding—suddenly disappear, and are replaced by a dark surrealism that was always promised but never delivered by *Anti-Oedipus*. Still the same language of desiring-production—signification and subjectification— but suddenly it becomes a different artistic model: the fractal model of "white walls/black holes" for a world invested by crash materialism.

Not a parallel opposition between *A Thousand Plateaus* and *Anti-Oedipus*, but a strange labyrinth of signs and bodies, where schizoids exist to confirm paranoic investments in their disappearing positions, and where desiring-production vanishes because nobody is interested any longer in production or desire for that matter. And not even libidinal investments, but anti-libidos of black holes and white walls. A *Thousand Plateaus*, then, as the Nietzschean truthsayer of the failure of the repressive psychoanalytical hypotheses of *Anti-Oedipus*: that point where the machinic values of capitalism disappears into cynical power. Where, that is, the comfortable image of the modernist Kant of determinism versus freedom (and all the secure bourgeois antinomies of *Anti-Oedipus*) disappear into the crash Kant of perspectival simulacra. Here things are interesting only when they float: an abstract machine of faciality, bodies without organs. Consequently, not *A Thousand Plateaus* as simply a dark region of oppressive schizoid signs and "intensive flows," but as the really existing material condition of hyper-modernism.

The basic political claim of Deleuze and Guattari in *Anti-Oedipus* that "things coexist" is profoundly mistaken.[15] In *A Thousand Plateaus*, nothing coexists, except in the degraded form of political illusion, a trompe l'oeil to deflect the eye from the irreality of serial disappearances, such as the disappearance of identity (into the "abstract machine of faciality"), of history (into the "regime of gestural signs"), of perspective (into the proto-surrealism of "white walls/black holes"), of bodies (into the "intensities" of decoded organs), and of subjectivity ("persons don't exist," only vibrations, knots, relays or connections).

In other words, the fatal destiny of the repressive hypothesis of *Anti-Oedipus* is completed, and then undermined, in the sacrificial violence of *A Thousand Plateaus*. The "false subjectivity" of oedipalization, with its valorization of the primitive "desire" of the happy schizoid is *doubled* in the blank significations of *A Thousand Plateaus*. Here, Nietzsche is brought on stage to mock the "grammatical error" of Kant, the sustaining modernist (and anti-bourgeois) belief that conditions of preservation are predicates of existence. For Deleuze and Guattari's confession can be so brilliant, not just because it is so deeply mistaken, but because they work with the materiality of their fatal error (the repressive themes of *Anti-Oedipus*), to make of *A Thousand Plateaus* an ecstatic confession of the impotence of the materialist hypothesis.

For in reality, things do not co-exist. They do not even double, but work to exterminate one another in a fatal regression of sign-slides. The co-existence of all the big antinomies (Deleuze and Guattari's fabled "co-extensivity" as Kant's "synthetic apperceptions") is a fatal trompe l'oeil, a "delusional hypothesis," by which conditions of preservation can be presented as predicates of existence. Kant knew this. That is why he wrote the *Critique of Judgement* as an intellectual sleight-of-hand to deflect the moral attention of the legislative subject from the fatal impossibility of the first two *Critiques*; impossible, that is, except as manifestations of the cynical sign of the will to power. Nietzsche knew this. That is why the arc of a dead power traced out in *The Will to Power* is a grammatical exercise in preserving *us* from the sacrificial nihilism of the fatal sign-slide at the disappearing centre of things. And, in the end, Deleuze and Guattari know this too, which is why their epochal confession ends up by so brilliantly cancelling itself, like an Aesopian fable of the snake that consumes itself. A crash scene for the burnout of capital (into cynical power), desiring-production (into affectlessness), Oedipus (into sex in ruins—an abstract machine of sexuality for the flagging male penis), signification (into a topology of fatal signs), and of materialism into the radical immateriality of fractal topologies.

Perhaps it might well be said that if the writings of Deleuze and Guattari are horizoned by Nietzsche and Kant, then *A Thousand Plateaus* might be viewed as the "will to power" which emerges in this century as the truth-sayer of the three "Critiques" of *Anti-Oedipus*. The confession of Deleuze and Guattari, therefore, as really a mimetic enactment of the ruins of sacrificial culture. A degree-zero point in the labyrinth, where differential intensities meet, only to breakthrough, breakdown and burnout in an indefinite proliferation of cynical signs. It becomes a confession, then, of materialism in ruins.

Romantic Mysticism

Deleuze and Guattari's thought is infected with romantic mysticism, with, that is, "becoming" as its defining monism: becoming-animal, becoming-intense, becoming-woman, becoming-dog, becoming-vegetable, becoming-stars.

Not satisfied like Baudrillard or Barthes to simply be barometers of experience, the thought of Deleuze and Guattari is either *of their situation*, or it does not exist. Not a materialism of externalities, but a dirty materialism, that operates at the violent edge of the "molar" (the determinism of our biological and historical circumstance) and the "molecular" (the blasting away of the dead weight of the molar by the *virtual experience of becoming)*; and that can be so dramatic because it inscribes in poetic imagination the actual feeling of being born under the gravitational weight of a "body with organs" and with a fixed subjectivity, of *being molar* as our first involuntary act. In their writing, the immanence of the body with organs drags us down to an inevitable destiny with determinism.

It is to break this tyranny of the molar, to provide the dead weight of materialism with a creative principle of internal renewal that the romantic mysticism of *becoming* must be imported. And it is! Like Heidegger's "lightning flash" which illuminates for an instant the oppressiveness of the metaphysic of Being, the horizon of materialism clears and a new dancing subjectivity suddenly appears.

> You are longitude and latitude, a set of speeds and slownessess between unformed particles, a set of nonspecified affects. You have the individuality of a day, a season, a year, *a life* (regardless of its duration)—a climate, a wind, a fog, a swarm, a pack (regardless of its regularity). Or at least you can have it, you can reach it.[16]

> It is the entire assemblage in its individuated aggregate that is a haecceity; it is this assemblage that is defined by a longitude and a latitude, by speeds and affects, independently of forms and subjects, which belong to another plane. It is the wolf itself, and the horse, and the child, that cease to be subjects to become events, in assemblages that are inseparable from an hour, a season, an atmosphere, an air, a life. The street enters into composition with the air, and the beast and the full moon enter into composition with each other... Haecceity, fog, glare. A haecceity has neither beginning nor end, origin nor destination; it is always in the middle. It is not made of points, only of lines. It is a rhizome.[17]

Everything in Deleuze and Guattari's thought rushes towards a fateful encounter with Spinoza. And why not? His *Ethics*, or more pertinently his essay, "On the Improvement of the Understanding,"[18] is the revelatory principle, the theology of hope, that is introjected into the inertial world of materialism as a new synthetic principle of unity, and of creative regeneration. Deleuze and Guattari are explicit about this:

> *Memories of a Spinozist, I.* Substantial or essential forms have been critiqued in many different ways. Spinoza's approach is radical: Arrive at elements that no longer have either form or function, that are abstract in this sense even though they are perfectly real. They are

distinguished solely by movement and rest, slowness and speed. They are not atoms, in other words, finite elements still endowed with form. They are infinitely small, ultimate parts of an actual infinity, laid out on the same plane of consistency or composition. They are not defined by their number since they always come in infinities...(E)ach individual is an infinite multiplicity, and the whole of nature is a multiplicity of perfectly individuated multiplicities. The plane of consistency of nature is like an immense Abstract Machine, abstract yet real and individual...[19]

Memories of a Spinozist, II. There is another aspect to Spinoza. To every relation of movement and rest, speed and slowness grouping together an infinity of parts, there corresponds a degree of power. To the relations composing, decomposing, or modifying an individual there correspond intensities that affect it, augmenting or diminishing its power to act; these intensities come from external parts or from the individual's own parts. Affects are becomings. Spinoza asks: What can a body do? We call the *latitude* of a body the affects of which it is capable at a given degree of power, or rather within the limits of that degree. *Latitude is made up of intensive parts falling under a capacity, and longitude of extensive parts falling under a relation.* In the same way we avoided defining a body by its organs and functions we will avoid defining it by Species or Genus characteristics; instead we will seek to count its affects. This kind of study is called ethology, and this is the sense in which Spinoza wrote a true Ethics.[20]

So then, the perilous seduction of the new age in the triumphant form of a theology of "affects." No longer individuality governed by the symbolic order of the metaphysics of Being, but the possessed individual as a process of "affects," "assemblages," and "haecceities:" the hyper-body of the new age, that is, as a kind of "fog, glare." A perfect description, in short, of the *virtual body*, of the *virtual self*: the self which has no real corporeal existence, only an affective existence as a temporary, always mobile, almost mathematical, site for the remapping of experience. Here, the body with organs is finally left behind as we take flight into the bloated abstract belly of the society of operations. Not corporeality but the "body without organs," not Being but becoming, not Species, but "machinic assemblages;" not the inert dualism of nature/culture, body/imagination, but the *romance of the doubling.*[21]

This is not a new story, but a very old one: for what is the romantic mysticism of "becoming" but a retelling, this time in the language of emancipation not domination, of the story of the scientific imagination. The impossible dream, that is, of escaping mortality, of evading the senescence of the body, by the construction of a virtual world: a world of "haecceities"—pure relational affects—governed by the monism of *becoming*. And not a happy dream either, but one which is motivated, as Nietzsche knew, by vicious *ressentiment* over the failure of the bodily organs to achieve immortality. It is not a story of freedom, but as Foucault once said, actually a story of the seduction of the language of domination and of the impossibility of transgression: the lightning-flash that illuminates the horizon only to reveal the immensity of the darkness within.

A hallucinatory theory, then, which hides the rotting nihilism within in the purified language of a new theology of hope: a political dispensation that seeks to suppress knowledge of the senescence of the body by thinking the virtual self as freedom. Spinoza, therefore, as the revelatory principle for the new age of romantic mysticism. The "theology of becoming" is the form that nihilism assumes in the age of virtual technology.

There is much to be learned from thought in ruins. This is what makes reading Deleuze and Guattari such a fascinating, and ultimately rewarding, exercise, for in their imagination a searing description of the tattooed body as a basic datum of virtual reality is to be discovered. This is not thought *about* technology nor, for that matter, *about* the body. It is, instead, a thought-body and a thought-technology: a writing which can be so compelling because it actually *is* what it only purports to describe: "becoming virtual." In this theorization, the horizon within which we are enfolded in technological society is rehearsed in chilling terms.

Much better than Foucault, who understood that words are things, but who then took this insight to ground by focussing on technologies of speech, Deleuze and Guattari's is a reading of the tattooed body, the marking of the internal organs by a machinery of cynical power. Their's is a description of the hyper-modern individual: trapped within the heavy gravity of a body with organs, drained of its creative energies by the demands of historicized subjectivity; but always with the possibility of *becoming*: becoming-animal, becoming-woman, becoming-intense. Not simply the old tensions of "paranoic investments" and "schizoid breaks," but something new, a romance of the doubling as the essential feature of the virtual self.

This is the point, or should we say "line," where the great insights of relativity theory (virtual space) and the uncertainty principle (the self as a quantum fluctuation), of all the philosophical breakthroughs of those other scientific "nomads," from Einstein to Heisenberg, suddenly return from the natural galaxy to the social universe, to become the defining terms of what Deleuze and Guattari describe as "nomad" subjectivity. A *Thousand Plateaus* and their parallel works on Bacon, Kant, and Kafka are descriptions drawn straight from postmodern physics, from its "improved understanding" of the virtual self. In fact, this is is exactly what Deleuze and Guattari have theorized: the *regulatory axiomatics of the virtual self*. With this difference. They merge the postmodernism of quantum mechanics with the poststructuralism of molecular biology: the transmutation of a relational world of pure affects and intensities— longitutudes and latitudes, speeds and slownesses—into a micro-physics of the animal kingdom. Perfect vegetable consciousness: the "rhizomatic" network projects the heretofore low epistemological profile of the strawberry patch into the regulatory principle of the individual and society as a multiplicity of lines of flight and departure. Or, might it be said, rhizomes only follow the vegetative mathematics of fractals, of the virtual space of dispersions and curvature. Not the "symbolic oedipal community" as the "plane of organization" of the virtual self, but *becoming* as its "plane of consistency"; not the "striated" space of the despotic state, but the "smooth surfaces" of the virtual self; and most certainly not the language of breaks and ruptures, but a cabalism of alchemical vegetative transformations.[22] The virtual self, therefore, as a musical composition, a mathematical configuration, an atmospheric effect. A truly enchanted kingdom of romantic mysticism: with Spinoza as its leading theologian, Kafka's "metamorphosis" as its principle of alchemical mutation, the virtual self as its transcendent ideal, the strawberry patch as its material reality, and becoming as its revelatory moment.

Panic Doublings/Panic Materialism

The romantic mysticism of Spinoza's ethics, with its seduction of becoming, is the panic principle which makes Deleuze and Guattari's thought possible. Materialism in the new age, therefore, is all about panic doublings: the flight from the body with organs to the digital dreams of becoming-speed, becoming-slownesses; and the fantastic valorization of the virtual self by the fear of falling back into corporeality, into the body with (dying) organs. The doubling, then, of a future of delusional desire and a past of fear as the "blink" at the disappearing centre of new age materialism. The language of panic doubling, therefore, recapitulates at a higher level of abstraction and generality the more classical discourse of liberalism. It is a political discourse of panic materialism which is not that dissimilar from the Lockean fear of death, and which motivated in turn its own search for the first of all the virtual selves: the bourgeois subject of the pursuit of happiness, property rights, and the avoidance of death. This time we are not present at the birth of the bourgeois subject, however, but in the more melancholy era of Locke, the bourgeois subject, of modernist doubling all in ruins. Yet, from the ruins of the bourgeois subject there stirs again in Deleuze and Guattari's thought the first timid motions of an old siren-call: the reconstitution of the dynamic will to will of the post-bourgeois subject, the virtual subject, on the basis of the liquid doubling of fear (of immanence) and desire (of transcendence). What is this but the triumphant reassertion of the ideolect of the post-liberal subject, all the more persuasive for its transgressionary appeal? Consequently, a materialist theory that only works to confirm what it thought it was finally rupturing: that is, the idea of the impossibility of the materialist subject except as an optical after-image of the hippie monism of romantic mysticism. What Nietzsche once described as the vicious "prejudices" which obscure the nihilism within.

Anyway, Why fear? and Why desire? No one is grimmer than Deleuze and Guattari on the colonization of subjectivity by despotic capitalism. Their works are about the tattooed body. About the "markings" of the body, its organs, its gestures, its language by a circulating power. Foucault might have ventured onto this terrain of a relational power, but it was only to immediately suppress his fatal insight by a turn to a theory of speech, to a "power without a sex," to a language without roots. Not, though, for Deleuze and Guattari. Refusing the post-Cartesian inhibitions of the "language subordination" of post-structuralism, they went all the way by writing, that is, a schizo-philosophy of the tattooed body. Tattooed not just on the outside (although that too), but on the inside: a signatured body written where semiology acquires corporeality, where the sign finally breathes, taking possession of the bodily organs it thought it was only denoting from afar.

To read Deleuze and Guattari's writings on the tattooed body—and they have never written anything else— is really to finally understand Nietzsche: to be in the presence of the "ascetic priest" of *On the Genealogy of Morals*, ministering doses of sacrificial violence to the scapegoat-lust of the passive nihilists; to understand oedipalization, not as a psychoanalytical theory, but as an advanced and decompositive stage in the politics of ressentiment; to finally know cynical power as the dark infinity of schizoanalysis; and to recognize the masochism of *Coldness and Cruelty* as doppelganger to Nietzsche's suicidal nihilists.[23] To meditate, that is, on the tattooed body with its impossible doubling of fear and desire as the (already colonized) limits of subjectivity in virtual reality.

And it is to recognize as well the deep affinity between feminism and the rhizomatic perspective of Deleuze and Guattari. For what has feminist theory always been about if not a refusal of the grand metaphysics of Being, of the unitary male subject, of the phallocentric order of the Subject, Species, and Membership; in favor a world of "multiplicities," of a dancing materiality of lines of flight and departure; of a world reenchanted by the language of desire? Not the old boring world of phallocentric oppositions, but liquid doublings where the body finally speaks, where alchemy is the rule, and where the terrestial kingdom of *grounded* consciousness—the vegetative spatiality of the rhizomatic net-work—finally usurps abstract univocal perspective. Where, that is, a new language is articulated which is capable of addressing both the disappearance of women under the sign of despotic power: the material language of markings, of deterritorialization and dematerialization, of gestural signatures; and of inscribing a new feminist possibility: the subject as "longitudes and latitudes, speeds and slownesses, moments of intensity." The feminist subject, then, as an event-scene, living at the edge of the material body and virtual reality. Neither really pure corporeal denotation or perfect virtuality or desire; but both simultaneously. A "virtual feminism" which is a matter of decodings (the "multiplicities" in the relational world of the virtual self) and resignifications (the re-enchantment of bodily desire). Does this mean, therefore, that virtual feminism is the first and leading subject of post-liberalism? or that the doubling of the body in virtual reality is the transgression which transforms the world of digital reality? Or might it mean simply that, as Deleuze and Guattari might insist, "virtual feminism" is also a "plateau:" a momentary line of arrival and departure for those womanly nomads in search of the body doubled?

Refusing (Baudrillard's) Skepticism

Deleuze and Guattari are on the opposite side of the French mind from the radical skepticism, represented by Baudrillard and Barthes.

Baudrillard focusses on the disappearing cultural space of the real and the counterfeit, only to project its violent implosion into simulation and thereupon into fractal subjectivity. Against the order of simulation, Deleuze and Guattari want to recover the possibility of the rematerialization of experience: a rhizomatic network of experience where events vanish into a decoded world of immateriality, only to instantly reappear in their opposite sign form in an endless chain of "lines" of flight and interruption.[24] Barthes might have thought through the empire of the sign to its abstract locus in cynical power, but Deleuze and Guattari want to go beyond the semiurgical language of the sign to a biological theory of homeostatic exchanges. Baudrillard theorizes psychoanalysis under the sacrificial sign of seduction; whereas Deleuze and Guattari force Freud's theory of oedipalization into the colonializing language of a social "repression-hypothesis." Barthes's thought traces a great arc of reversal from a materialist science of the sign (*The Fashion System*) to a tragic sense of radical skepticism (*Barthes by Barthes*), but Deleuze and Guattari work to reinvigorate the materialist eschatology. At first, with a hyper-Kantian theory of "capitalist axiomatics" (*Anti-Oedipus*) and then with the injection of the dark tradition of nomadic thought (Nietzsche, Artaud, Spinoza) into the society of pure signification. Both Barthes and Baudrillard ultimately refuse the modernist dualisms—Barthes in favor of an austere sense of the empire of the cynical sign and Baudrillard in favor of a bitterly nostalgic sense of seduction—but Deleuze and Guattari struggle to revive a liquid materialism, one which preserves the honour of the "doubling." That is, their theorization of doublings, signification/ subjectification, recuperates the legacy of naturalism in hyper-modern form.

Not everything is, however, dissimilar. Barthes's machinery of cynical rhetoric, formulated in his early proto-materialist period, parallels Deleuze and Guattari's rhizomatic network. In addition Baudrillard's epochal description of the "mirror of production" has its brilliant counterpart in their description of the abstract machinery of libidinal capitalism in *Anti-Oedipus*.

What is really revived in the incipient debate of Deleuze and Guattari against Baudrillard and Barthes is less, perhaps, a division of contemporary French thought on the subjectivity of the possessed individual, than a more classical reprise of two paradigmatic viewpoints on the human condition: romanticism and skepticism. It is not, however, a simple struggle between classical romanticism rooted in a pragmatic faith in naturalism as the limit of experience and a classical skepticism which submits experience to a decompositive logic, but between hyper-romanticism and hyper-skepticism. Hyper-romanticism? That's a post-romantic viewpoint that can be excessive in its claims because it runs at the violent edge of total subjectification and total signification. And not in a static way, but a libidinal romanticism which makes experience float in a series of mystical doublings ("thousand plateaus"), where all experience mutates in a chain of vegetable-like cabalisms (metal turns into labor; money mutates into air). A world under the alchemical sign of Kafka, Spinoza and Nietzsche where naturalism is so pure, intense, suffocating, and cynical that it can only be voided by the re-enchantment promised by romantic mysticism. And hyper-skepticism? That's rationalism in its purest form: fractal experience, and fractal subjectivity too, so oppressive that it collapses into its own fatal abyss—the return of symbolism, magic and irrationality. The hyper-romantic is a world of failed nostalgia dissolving into bitterness, a skeptical universe, which can only be restimulated by the primitivist sacrificial violence of its own necrophilic myths: dead seduction, history, society, and dead subjectivity.

Two habits of mind, then, which are deeply contestational because each is derived from a different ontology (naturalism versus rationalism), an opposing epistemology (hyper-mysticism versus hyper-sociolectics), a competing axiology (pragmatic materialism versus simulation) and a contrasting aesthetics (thousand plateaus versus fractal subjectivity). While the fate of the skeptical viewpoint is always the same, the impossible dream of "seduction" (Baudrillard) or the "empire of the sign" (Barthes) as the vanishing points where nostalgia goes to die in bitterness, so too is the fate of romanticism proscribed. Lacking any *internal* principle of creative regeneration to reenergize the inert, and always flagging, world of materialism, the romantic viewpoint must import a synthetic principle of unity from the *outside*. Hyper-romanticism must devolve into the seductive, because so perilous, language of mysticism. In the end, it must be religious in order to provide a theological dispensation for a materialist experience where as Nietzsche once said: "Truth is dead, everything is permitted."[25]

Today, the criticism of Baudrillard's skepticism is relentless and furious, particularly from cultural materialists. Indeed, if we take Foucault's dead body as a common sacrificial table of French values, then it is noteworthy that Baudrillard, who honored Foucault in *Oublier Foucault* by following the Nietzschean prescription that concluded *Madness and Civilization* (honor thinkers by doing their thought violence, by making them bend, and crackle and complain under the weight of your own insistent questions), was not invited by Paris intellectuals, Foucauldian materialists all, to speak or even attend his memorial service.

In defence of Baudrillard, and against Deleuze and Guattari, I would say this. That Baudrillard's most infuriating quality, his unrelenting melancholy skepticism, has saved him from theology, from the ultimately futile search for a revelatory principle—the "new romanticism," the "new historicism." Not so for Deleuze and Guattari whose philosophy is more innocent, and historically naive, because it still has faith in "doublings," in irruptions, gestures, ruptures, and lines of flight and departure. If it does not suffer from the world weariness which infects Baudrillard (and which shields him from anything but grimly realistic, skeptical meditations on the political event-scenes that mark the dying days of the twentieth-century), then it also does not have his haunted understanding of the naturalist delusion. Deleuze and Guattari have not yet thought through, in all of its elemental ferocity, the terrible thought that doublings, most of all, mark the impossibility of transgression, that doublings are the social mechanism by which the limit experience (Kant's "predicates of existence" as conditions of preservation) works to save itself. They have not yet begun to understand the Nietzsche of *The Will to Power* or of *Thus Spake Zarathustra*: the Nietzsche who could say of materialism that it is a "will to nothingness," part, that is, of the seductive appeal of the "ascetic ideal."

...a will running counter to life, a revolt against the most fundamental presuppositions of life; yet it is and remains a *will*! And, to repeat at the end what I said in the beginning: rather than want nothing, man even wants nothingness.[26]

It must also be said, however, that all of Deleuze and Guattari's thought struggles to keep alive the memory of tortured subjectivity. Their theory is a gamble on subjectivity as an unfinished project, on turnings, on the self as a multiplicity of possibile beginnings and endings. They may be historically naive, and for that matter work to re-enchant a materialism that is itself part of the sacrificial logic of the ascetic ideal, but they are emotionally correct. Is it possible that critical politics today—the recuperation of *difference* against the white walls of the society of pure signification—is only possible on the basis of the naturalist delusion: the mistaken faith in the romantic mysticism of doublings? Does politics demand a revelatory principle for its operation? And if this is the case, might it be said then that the last contribution of Deleuze and Guattari is less philosophical, psychological, or literary than neo-proletarian. Migrant thinkers, that is, who have written across the text of signification the prejudices necessary to political dissent: architects of a "dirty materialism" who have thought through the materialist subject to its beckoning horizon of separation, who have charted out the path of an internal migration—a nomadic journey—beyond the culture of instrumental signification.

If Spinoza is their breakdown, he is also their breakthrough. And if romantic mysticism is ultimately doomed as a politics of material dissent, then in that failure may yet be found an alchemical purchase on an older dream of an older age: the dream of a thousand plateaus, beyond coldness and cruelty.

Spinoza in Ruins

This inmost essence must be sought solely from fixed and eternal things, and from the laws, inscribed (so to speak) in those things as in their true codes, according to which all particular things take place and are arranged; nay, these mutable particular things depend so intimately and essentially upon the fixed things, that they cannot either be or be conceived without them.

Spinoza, "On the Improvement of the Understanding"

All of Deleuze and Guattari's writings are a confession of the failure of materialism, the vanishing of the real material subject into sacrificial violence: the despot god needs the recurrent image of the goat's ass, the face only exists as an empty plateau of signification, technologies function as apparatuses of "machinic enslavement" where the subject is reduced to a "part," a "servomechanism" of the ruling axiomatic. A whole fascinating scene of the vanishing of materialism into seduction, of the disappearance of subjects into technical prosthetics, of the disintegration of the sign into a rhizomatic network of virtual lines, without beginning or ending.

It does not help at all that Deleuze and Guattari attempt to take cover under the sign of Spinoza's *Ethics*. Read Spinoza, not just the *Ethics*, but his really elemental text, "On the Improvement of the Understanding," which provides the code of the ethics to follow. This is not a story of romanticism, mysticism, naturalism, of the creation of a "new principle," but the reverse. It is the story of the ruling illusions of naturalism, where the will to understanding also contains the fatal defect of the will to power: the transformation of purely grammatical attitude into a metaphysics of human experience.

Perhaps Deleuze and Guattari have never been interested in Spinoza at all. Maybe they were always secretly fascinated by the dream of Spinoza in ruins. Maybe Spinoza had for them a purely psychoanalytical function, a screen-mechanism, a trompe l'oeil, within which they repressed their own attraction to the world of sacrificial materialism: the masochistic universe of *Coldness and Cruelty*. In this case, a second hypothesis is necessary: the writings of Deleuze and Guattari as a fantastic piling up of the debris of romanticism: parodic texts which accumulate the dead desires of the post-romantic subject, only to subvert the "will to desire" by showing its moment of sacrificial cancellation. Here, bodies only exist as sites of decoded organ-plays, facialization is the signifying regime par excellence, power mutates into the death of desire, and even capitalism reverts to the archaic sign of despotism. And Spinoza? He exists in their texts only in negative form. Not, as Foucault would have it, as the progenitor of a new ethics, but as the sublimation of ethics into another manifestation of the will to power. Not Spinoza as the creator of a "new principle," but as the religious spokesperson of a more ancient theme: the reversion at the very inception of Enlightenment to the naturalistic illusion of that other enlightenment, the Greek enlightenment of classical times, where it also was believed that nature could provide a creative principle of regeneration. It was just from the dashed historical hopes of this more ancient expression of naturalism that Christianity finally emerged with a response to the problem that naturalism could never resolve: How, that is, to make of experience its own synthetic principle of unity, without having to rely on an external revelatory moment—an imported "new principle"—to hold the material world together? Spinoza knew that naturalism never had anything to do with directly experienced nature nor with materialism, for that matter, but that the conflict was about the imposition of the "will to nature," the "will to understanding" onto a recalcitrant human history.

"On the Improvement of the Understanding" is a grisly text. Published in 1632, it reads like a primer of the fin de millennium, that fateful moment when, for a single instant, the epistemological strategy of a nihilistic western civilization let down its guard, permitting us to improve *our* understanding of the conceptual prison-house within which *we* would be enfolded as our technological horizon. There are no ethics, only a happy conjunction of the ethical imperative with cynical power; no nature, only understanding; no "new principle," only the story of materialism in ruins; and no materialism either, only a "covergence of mind and nature."

To meditate upon "On the Improvement of the Understanding" is to enter deeply into the world of Spinoza as simulacrum. Everything is there: an *essentialist* ontology that is based on a primal act of faith in the "method of reflective knowledge" as the way of "possessing subjectively, nature's essence, order and union;" a *self-actional* epistemology that reduces human experience to a reified conception of "the understand-ing" ("the true method of discovery is to form thoughts from some given definition") for its interpretation; a *canonical* axiology, which refuses "fictions, doubts and falsehood" in favour of a theory of society driven by the will to truth; and a *virtual* aesthetics that seeks the harmonization of "pure intellect" and pure "essences or proximate causes" ("the properties of things are not understood so long as their essences are unknown...").

Spinoza's "understanding" represents that fateful moment when the will to religious belief combines with the (postivistic) will to truth. Not truth simply as representative of a preexistent religious faith, nor truth in relationship to a co-existing material reality, but something much more ominous: *the emergence of cynical truth.* Spinoza's "understanding," that is, as its own doubled signifier: part metaphor/part metonymy; part revelatory/part nominalistic; part "method of reflective knowledge"/part essentialist locus of its own subordination (of experience) to "pure intellect." What of the ethics of cynical truth as its own doubled signifier? A double ethics follows: the ethics of rationalist exclusion (of the "chaotic and irrational" universe of "fictions, falsities and doubts"); and the ethics of inclusion (the remaking of the universe according to the convergence of mind and nature in the simulacrum of "pure intellect").

Spinoza takes us back once more to the ethics of the hangman, to that troubling meeting of the will to truth and the will to justice in the western mind. An ethics that can be very compelling because it masquerades as materialistic only to disappear experience under the sign of a double moment of reification; and because it reverses the meaning of rationality. No longer rationality in relation to the "fictions, falsities and doubts" of the history of human experience, but a cold rationalism that links its fate to the strategies of instrumental signification. An ethics, then, without fictions because it introduces *us* to a new carceral of truth, without falsities because it is spoken in the language of the simulacrum of pure intellect; and without doubt because it is based on the religious vocation of the "method of discovery" of essences.

Might it be that in identifying their perspective so closely with Spinoza's carceral ethics, with the primal of the *will to truth*, that Deleuze and Guattari are also telling us that their thought can take its place without a ripple of discontent nor a murmur of equivocation in a pattern of western thought that extends from Spinoza and Bacon to the most relentless positivisms of the twentieth-century? Is it possible that their final reversal is a purely sacrificial one: the production of a "lite materialism" as the dynamic form that rationalism assumes today? Is it possible, just possible, that in their works we find the fulfillment of Spinoza's architectural dream:

> The more ideas express perfection of any object, the more perfect are they themselves; for we do not admire the architect who has planned a chapel so much as the architect who has planned a spendid temple.
> Spinoza, "On the Improvement of the Understanding"

Becoming-Crash (Scenes)

What if we were to take Deleuze and Guattari at their word? To actually rethink the world in terms of virtual reality. Becoming virtual, although not within the symbolic order of romanticism, and most certainly not under the illusion that the pataphysics of becoming opposes in any fundamental way the metaphysics of Being, but of romanticism on its cold side. Not its romantic mystical side—the new sublime of "haecceity"— but on its chilled-eyed side, where becoming virtual heats up, accelerates, and then crashes to its point of imminent collapse.

Deleuze and Guattari, then, as theorists par excellence of *becoming-crash*, the first philosophers of romantic skepticism. Not a new world of a "thousand plateaus," but of a thousand crash scenes: all alchemical mutations, all event-scenes, all purely mathematical instances of longitudes and latitudes, speeds and slownesses, points of intensive duration. Not "machinic assemblages" but crash machines, not "smooth surfaces" but broken events, and certainly not power functioning any longer as a "plane of organization" (as opposed to the "plane of consistency" of virtual space) or "striated space" (against the "rhizomatic" space of abrupt lines of departure and arrival). Power does not act that way anymore, and maybe it never has. The metaphysics of Being always, then, as a trompe l'oeil, camouflaging the real existence of virtual power: power as a site of becoming-cynical, a sign of that which never has existed except as a perspectival simulacrum. So then, becoming on its dark and imploded side: a zone of becoming crash-scenes. And all this perfectly faithful to Deleuze and Guattari who urge us to make of their texts disappearing moments of pure virtuality.

So then, six sites of *becoming-crash (scenes)* as the truth-sayer of the fatal destiny—Nietzsche's "rotting nihilism"—of virtual reality. The method of romantic skepticism, therefore, as decompositive of the purely spatialized universe of virtual reality. Consequently, the return of paranoic investment is the point of imminent reversability of the perilous seduction of the new age of schizoanalysis.

Becoming-Michael Jackson's Collapsing Nose

> The face is the Icon proper to the signifying regime, the
> reterritorialization internal to the system... The signifier is always
> facialized.

> Not only is language always accompanied by faciality traits, but the
> face crystallizes all redundancies, it emits and receives, releases and
> recaptures signifying signs. It is a whole body unto itself; it is like the
> body of the center of significance to which all of the deterritorialized
> signs affix themselves, and it marks the limits of their deterritorialization.
> Deleuze and Guattari, *A Thousand Plateaus*

Probably because he takes Franz Fanon's analysis of race as a purely
accidental quality so seriously, Michael Jackson's image construct has
gone for a complete make-over: bleached skin, retooled eyes, oxygen
pumped organs, and a sculpted nose as cute and pert as the young Diana
Ross's. The earth-bound body of the smallest member of the *Jackson 5*
has disappeared and what has taken its place is a random image museum
culled from Disney's Peter Pan.

There is one big problem, however. Michael Jackson's nose is
collapsing, actually deflating, as the surgically implanted cartilage wilts
under the pressure of earthly gravitation. Probably because it was
designed solely as an image construct for liquid proliferation across the
mediascape, Jackson's humanoid nose has been quickly brought to
ground by the G-forces of earthly space. The body recut and redesigned
for immediate satellization in the real world of TV, the world's first *living*
perfectly preserved body, begins to implode under the inertial drag of
gravity waves. The collapsing nose, then, as a postmodern version of
Freud's return of the repressed. The exterminated body of the *Jackson 5*
returning as fleshly memory to haunt the irreality of the cultural icon of
Michael Jackson

So then, one further transgression in the sacrifice of the Jackson body.
Why not do away with the nose altogether, pump up the skin syntheti-
cally to a perfect transparency, energize the eyes to glistening flares, and
find another media representation for those wonderful dancing legs?
Which is, of course, exactly what the Jackson humanoid has done. In a
recent press release out of MTV, Jackson has announced that he has now

disappeared into a dancing Raisin commercial (without the wrinkles), an advertisement where a dancing raisin takes Michael's place in a perfect dance simulation. The collapsing nose, therefore, as a prelude to Michael Jackson's final disappearance into a California raisin, just drying in the sun.

Becoming-Sacrificial Art

I only exist to consume other people's art. That is the triumphant slogan of the possessed individual. No longer the romantic solitary ego of the post-romantics, and certainly not a floating id, the possessed individual exists under the sign of abuse value. An object of appropriation to such an extent that its identity is invested by the excremental matter of consumption. Thus, Bataille as the privileged theorist of appropriation and excretion:

> The process of simple appropriation is normally presented within the process of composite excretion, insofar as it is necessary for the production of an alternating rhythm, for example in the following passage from Sade:

> Verneuil makes someone shit, he eats the turd, and then demands that someone eat his. The one who eats the shit vomits; he devours her puke.[27]

Sacrificial consumption, then, as the excremental phase of appropriation: i.e., when the object appropriated is devoured by the will to power. Sade's Verneuil is the art critic whose will to judgement consists only of the elemental and excremental act of making someone shit, eating their turd, and demanding that someone eat his.

Or is it just the reverse? Not the art critic as Sade's Verneuil, but as the emblematic cultural form of the repression of denial. Art criticism as consumption with such violent intensity that the excremental aspect of appropriation is elided:

> I only exist
> I only exist to consume
> I only exist to consume other people
> I only exist to consume other people's art

Art as the ultimate object of aestheticization of the excremental act of appropriation. Here, all the elemental signs of the chain of secretion and excretion are denied under the abstract code of the will to judgement. Art criticism, then, as possession of the excrementia of the body of the artist.

Anyway, what is art in the age of sacrificial culture? A sacramental (sacrificial) sign of homogeneity or an excretory symbol of heterogeneous production? Art as appropriation or exretion? Or both? Appropriation in the violent sense, in that art mutates the material order of reality into a spectral system of symbolic signs, and excretion to the extent that art is now the excretory phase of the most irreducible objects of production.

Does art represent now the most highly aestheticized phase of designer culture, or is the transmutation of art into the dominant sign of consumer society itself an excremental act of eating art? Eating art? That is the consumption of art as the violent appropriation of its own aesthetic sign by a predatory culture existing under the twin signs of excretion and appropriation. Here, the violent consumption of art as the decoded sign of designer culture is also an act of sacrificial renewal by the possessed individual.

Becoming-Crash Machines

In America today, even machines have gone hyper-modern. They exist at the edge of ecstasy and doom, sites of fantastic frenzy and inertia: Deleuzian technologies for an America that has vanished into its own schizoid machinery of abstract robotics.

When I was in Detroit recently, I was told by a guy in the UAW about General Motor's new all automated plant, which had to be shut down and abandoned because the robots, probably thinking about the Dance of Death in the Middle Ages, had suddenly mutinied and gone to frenzy. In this plant, the robots in the painting division had forgotten all about the cars and had began to compulsively paint themselves over and over again. In the welding division, the robots, caught up in a web of paranoic frenzy, were welding themselves and each other. And on the assembly lines, the robotic machines began ripping the doors off all the passing cars. Not an equivalence any longer between rationalization and automation, but hyper-modern corporations as real Bataillean scenes of cancellation, catastrophe, and exterminism.

It's the very same in the paper mill towns of northern Canada. In Red Rock, my hometown, a pulp and paper mill town on the northern shore of Lake Superior, I was told recently by my brother, a machinist, about how when the paper machines were attached to computers for programming, suddenly and unpredictably the computers—probably acting under the impact of French post-structuralism—would order the paper machines to speed up to escape velocity, to that ecstatic point where the machines would go flatline, spiralling massive twenty-ton rolls of paper hundreds of feet in the air. Just like in Don Delillo's *White Noise*, where when the plane is going down and all the passangers are panicking, the pilot comes on the PA to announce: "We're going down. We're going to crash. We're a gleaming, beaming death machine." Which was, of course, just what the stewardess said, recently, on a TWA flight out of Athens which was just bombed but managed to return to the airport. In her survivor report to the media, she said about the passengers during the crisis: "Everyone was screaming, everyone was taking pictures."

Anyway, we are probably already living in post-millennial consciousness on the other side of the Year 2000. We are the first human beings to live in the virtual space of a fatal attraction between postmodern science and popular culture. More than we may suspect, panic science is now the deepest language of consumption, entertainment, and information technology just as much as the oscillating fin de millennium mood of deep euphoria and deep despair of contemporary culture is the ruling ideology of postmodern science.

Becoming-crash machines, then, for the end of the world.

Becoming-the Velocity of Music

What is the speed of music? At what point does music red shift to ultrasonic velocity like all those spectral objects before it, break the sound barrier and then follow an immense curvature towards that point of an incredible sound density, where music can finally move at such violent speeds that it can no longer be heard, even by mutant membranes. The fatal point, that is, where music breaks beyond the speed of light, falling into a deep and immense silence.

Maximalism, as the composer Steve Gibson notes, is the name given to a new tendency in music today—entropy music—where, like early pioneers in jet aircraft technology, the aim is to evolve an improved eardrum for the mutant ear, a mutant membrane that can actually see the sound pressure of the velocity of music. Entropy music, then, as a dense configuration of sound-objects, each of which is pushed by sheer decibel strength to its ultimate pressure point, to that elusive point where music as a high velocity sound object breaks beyond the speed of light to shatter the old second-millennium ear drum, beyond 130 decibels like all those boom cars in Los Angeles.

Recently, the *New York Times* had this to say about boom cars:

> Young people are converting cars into rolling radio stations by stuffing them with dozens of speakers, disc jukeboxes, and amplifiers capable of booming rock and rap music at decibel levels powerful enough to rattle neighbour's windows, ruin their hearing and assault their captive audience.
>
> Those who compete in sound-competitions say the thump of a high-decibel stereo is addictive. You ask yourself: If 200 watts sound good, what will 400 watts sound like? As one car boomer says: "I'm young and stupid, I guess."

Not really cars any longer, but entropic sound chambers where the body curls up at the edge of 400 watts of rap music, folds outwards against the sound pressure, running finally at the edge of earth and sky. A perfect sound event-scene. Sky walking actually, mutating into a force field with thunders across the empty circulatory system of postmodern suburbs. And not drivers any longer, but zooming scenes of sound intensity, filling all the dead air with dead sound, and all those empty city dreams with bleeding eardrums for the body mutant.

Why the compulsive drive to immense volumes of sound? A techno-logical fascination with bad infinity, with the necessity to challenge dead space? Or an implosion of sound to that point of intensity where silence finally begins? Boom cars as alternating scenes of violent silence, like the eye of a tropical hurricane, and mobile war strategies which overwhelm the menace of dead air in all those lonely cars with noise as a pure force-field. Consequently, boom cars in L.A. as the last and best of all the urban nomads: sites of "longitude and latitude, speed and slowness," moments of passing intensity. Boom cars, then, as crash *haecceities*: event-scenes for becoming the velocity of music.

Becoming-Sampler Self

In this wonderful world as we drift aimlessly across the mediascape, floating among the debris of all the seductive objects of desire, voyeurs in the cultural boutiques of which our bodies are only random and transitory terminal points, like Barthes's voyeurs, Benjamin's *flaneurs*, or Deleuze and Guattari's nomads in the magic kingdom of signs where we see with our ears, we can finally know the terminal blast of music to be our very own lost object of desire, the field across which bodies are coded, tattooed and signified in an endless circulation of spectral emotions.

If music is so seductive today, that is because it finally delivers on the catastrophe that was always promised by the society of capitalism and schizophrenia. Music as interesting, therefore, only in its dark and implosive side, in that impossible space where music prefigures our own dissolution into a spectral impulse in the circulatory system of the mediascape. Not by its content—words are always only a *mise-en-scène*, deflecting the ear from the violent aesthetics of pure sound-objects that prefigure the aestheticization of our own bodies as consumed objects; and certainly not through the form of music—in the age of sampler machines, music composition is itself already a servomechanism of virtual technology. The fascination with music today lies in its violence as a force-field which scripts bodies analogically, codes emotions, processes designer subjectivities, and which rehearses our own existence as crash bodies, by its violent alternation as a scene of ecstasy and inertia.

Sounds appear from nowhere and they decay rapidly. They move across the field of our bodies, and then disappear. They have no real presence, only a virtual and analogical presence. Sounds without history and without referent.

Consider sampler music, where music is created through random appropriation of the static of the mediascape. A perfect model for the sampler self of hyper-modern society. Never really stable, never really localized, the sampler self is a transitory terminal point for fantasized histories and fabulous identities. A trajectory of hallucinatory possibilities, with no history to inhibit its future, no encrusted identity to suppress its desire, no bodily organs to undermine its contingency. Knowing no real because it is already only a simulation of hystericized memories, the sampler self marks an end to the lament for the lost order of history. Is the sampler self false consciousness? No, that would be only nostalgia. It's the real world of virtual subjectivity. The sampler self is a bodily sound-object, the first identity prefigured by music technology. Like sampler music, the sampler self traces a great cultural arc, wrapping itself in the changing fashions of the mediascape, mutating to the mood of its environment, always metamorphosing as a point of excess and hysteria in its cultural space.

Sampler music, therefore, as working according to the aesthetic practice of going beyond culture by going into it as deeply as possible. It functions to undermine meaning, by deterritorializing culture, by adding third and fourth orders of surplus signification to cultural phenomena, by speeding up the media to their point of sacrificial collapse.

Becoming-Counterfeit

To tell the truth, art must always be forgery—a perfect counterfeit. This is the secret of its fatal seduction, and the promise of its aesthetic destiny. Here, art only succeeds to the extent that it compels the disappearing order of the real—real subjects, real sex, real space—to vanish into a virtual world of perspectival simulacra. Art, then, as an enchanted simulation of trompe l'oeil.

To speak of art authenticity/art forgery is to tease out the hidden meaning of the seduction of art. For at the centre of art is a fatal sign-slide, a violent principle of imminent reversibility, where the opposing poles— figuration/simulation, territorialization of the code/reterritorialization of the referent—flip into one another, and suddenly vanish. An alchemy of sign mutations. Not so much, then, art authenticity/art forgery as competitors in a great modernist tableau, but as key signs of hyper-modern art. Art which is lived at the edge of a proto-surrealistic tension between the real counterfeit (the cultural space of the reality-principle) and the counterfeit real (art as a second and third order of virtuality). As Deleuze and Guattari state in A *Thousand Plateaus*, the vanishing centre of things is a seductive space of sacrificial violence—white walls/black holes, breakdowns/breakthroughs, paranoic investments/schizoid flows. A degree-zero point of sacrificial violence where the counterfeit in art only obscures the function of art as a desperate way of re-enchanting the dying energies of counterfeit reality. Forgery, then, as faithful aesthetic reproductions, perfect copies, of already second-order simulacra as if to indicate that in virtual reality only mimesis counts. Consequently, becoming counterfeit as a perfect act of cultural critique, an artistic mimesis, for a society where serial reproduction is the basic strategy of the counterfeit real.

Art, however, has always been about the aesthetic remapping of experience, which is why art today is neither about technology as predator nor technology as victim, but as minotaur-figure: simultaneously the aesthetic language of the "operational arts" of the war machine, and the critical language of the "counterfeit arts"— the sampler self, scratch video—which liberate us. Art, then, as a degree-zero point of struggle between two opposing tendencies in the virtual world of cyber-technology: the operational arts against the dirty arts. The dirty arts? That's art as a critical probe of technological society. Art as all about:

> Becoming *virtual* so as to undermine the operational arts.
> Becoming *scratch* so as to rupture the smooth and unbroken
> surface of simulation.
> Becoming *digital* so as to overwhelm the modernist *recit* of sound
> by laying down 400 tracks of music.
> Becoming *sampler* so as to colonize from within the dominant
> Icons of culture, and then to distort them.
> Becoming *authentic*, then, by becoming virtual: a shaministic art
> which wears the mask of technology in order to dispel its demonic
> presence as an operational art.

6

Libidinal Technology:
Lyotard in the New World

When I think of Jean-François Lyotard what first comes to mind is Moose Jaw, Saskatchewan, and even more so Rick Hancox's experimental film, *Moose Jaw*.[1] This association is entirely fitting since Lyotard prides himself on recovering local "minor voices" against hegemonic discourses, and on privileging "incommensurability," "incongruities," and "paradox" as key signs of the postmodern condition. This is only to say that beyond his brilliant writings on phenomenology and Marxism, beyond his retheorization of aesthetic theory, and even beyond the pragmatic ethics of all his "language games," Lyotard is, in the end, the author of a philosophical *Moose Jaw*, and the best of all the "moose boosters" for the spirit of pragmatism as the primal of the postmodern condition.

The Moose Jaw Postmodern

Rick Hancox's *Moose Jaw* is already a Canadian classic, not only in experimental film-making but also as a prophetic analysis and re-creation of the Canadian discourse. In this film, there is everything: Moose Jaw itself as a privileged scene for understanding the big crash that is postmodern society; a daring reversal of the practice of documentary film-making into a personal, and deeply existential, journey into the interiority of Hancox's own mind; and a seductive and violent reversal of all of the key categories of contemporary culture—nostalgia, childhood, voyeurism, and history. In Hancox's cinematic imagination, we are simultaneously at the end of all things—the ten-year period that the film traces parallels the economic decline of Moose Jaw—and at the very beginning of something new. A meeting-point of autobiography and history, Moose Jaw also speaks deeply and profoundly of absurdity as the very essence of the Canadian identity. Moose Jaw, then, as the first of the really existentialist cities where economic impossibility is met with stoicism, and sometimes with maniacal boosterism. A Don Quixote city on the prairies that likes to boast, "There's a Future in Our Past" and where, in a fit of promotional enthusiasm, a gigantic moose (vandalized with fluorescent red balls) is placed on the Trans-Canada highway (three miles outside of Moose Jaw), with the predictable result that passing tourists stop for the obligatory Canadian Moose statue shot (like the Goose in Wawa or the Big Nickel in Sudbury), and then immediately get back in their cars to zoom on to the next photo opportunity.

There's a Past in Our Future

Moose Jaw is not about Canada's past, but about its future, where all the people have finally fled but where the empty machinery of neon signs on Main Street still whirs on in an indefinite circulation of images; where the economy has disappeared, imploded, but the local "Moose Boosters" suddenly intensify their advertising efforts on behalf of Moose Jaw as a new economic mecca (the biggest gambling casinos for a new Las Vegas of the north, the biggest retirement centre, the biggest transportation museum); and where the Canadian passenger railway (the famous

Rick Hancox, *Moose Jaw*.

"Canadian") may have been terminated, but leaves in its wake powerful memory traces, a whole railway museum culture.

Everything here has its final destiny as a museum specimen. Not just the transportation paraphernalia, particularly the railroad cars with their frozen wax figures of conductor and passengers, but the abandoned and shuttered Eaton's store with its two mythic dead crows rotting on the floor ("One crow sorrow. Two crows joy..."); and even the disappearance of Temple Gardens into yet another empty parking lot with a flashing neon sign ("This building will soon be gone, but the memories linger on"). Nothing is safe from museumization. Western frontier houses are carted down the highway to the "Prairie Pioneer Village Museum." The school still operates, but half of its windows are bricked up as if in impatient anticipation.

When Hancox began the film ten years ago, there was a beautiful wooden sign in the railroad station that announced arrivals and departures of all the trains. By the summer of 1989, the very same sign had already made its retirement home as yet another fossilized item in the transportation museum. Indeed, even the film-maker (most of all?) is not safe from the virus of museumization. In the latter part of *Moose Jaw*,

Grayson Hall. Built in 1911-12 by Wm.Grayson. Renovated in 1983 by Devlin & Lowe Enterprises.

MOOSE JAW

There's a future in our past.

Produced for Heritage Day, 1984 by Heritage Canada's **Moose Jaw Main Street Project**

Rick Hancox, *Moose Jaw*.

Hancox actually becomes one of the wax figures in the railroad car in the museum, caught perfectly in the pose of the grotesque his face smeared against the window. Here, the museum has finally come inside; and the living bodies on the outside are only trompe l'oeil deflecting attention from their actual body possession by broken dreams, kitsch memory traces, and ghost stories from childhood.

Eating Moose Jaw

This is also a film about "eating Moose Jaw," about, that is, the disappearance of the contents of Moose Jaw, such as the detritus of the transportation industry, houses, signs, whole streets—into a cavernous museum of Western culture; and the disappearance of the identities of the "Moose Boosters" most of all into an always fictionalized past: dinosaurs with skin like throbbing gristle; reveries of what might have been (Hancox's father says that when he first arrived, "They called Main Street 'the flash'"); and panic schemes for what still might be—the revival of the Sulphur Springs for a new Banff on the prairies.

Perhaps it is just the opposite. Not Moose Jaw in ruins, but a thriving city that can be so intensely postmodern that it has passed into another qualitative stage of contemporary cultural experience— "bimodernism." Indeed, Hancox's *Moose Jaw* can be so seductive because it works by tracing a logic of imminent reversibility where all of the original signs are flipped. Thus, the signs of nostalgia are speed-processed at the beginning of the film almost as if to remind us that this is *not* a film about hystericized male kitsch (the old and boring search for boyhood dreams); and history (the shuttered buildings everywhere, and the Hopper-like Main Street) flips into always blinking tourist signs (long after the Grant Hall Hotel closed, its exterior neon signs still beamed, its telephones and lights functioned, and the rooms came alive at night, almost like the *Shining*); and the panoptic eye of the observing camera is, halfway through the film, itself put under surveillance by the buildings it thought it was recording. *Moose Jaw*, then, as a possessed city of dreams where all of the old binary oppositions of modern Canada suddenly lose their force, and begin to short-circuit.

Hancox is conscious of this, and early on in the film he signals his awareness. On the train going out West, he reads a book on Crash Theory. And just in time. For *Moose Jaw* does not exist in this film, except as a surrealistic site of the very first of Canada's crash cities. A panic scene, that is, of our processing through technology to such a point of intensity that the catastrophe begins to slow down, to become inertial, to a point where we seemingly live in slow motion. And why not? Because here the surest sign of the passing violence of technology is its final appearance as the aestheticization of culture—the implosion of the city of broken dreams into a big museum. If Hancox can look so frantically and so long (ten years) for childhood memories: of his mother (the scenes of Eaton's with the lost boy's voice, "Over here dear"); of his old home; of his friend (the musician in Hollywood/Mexican simulacra); of his landscape (the snow scenes), of the abandoned railway station; it is because there is nothing there. Hancox's *Moose Jaw* has only a cinematic existence now, an empty sign onto which can be transcribed all of the flotsam of empty memory traces and dead desires. The memories have vanished into the spectral blue of the prairie sky, and what is left is a body and a time, that of a Canadian film-maker, with no history, no autobiography, no determinate meaning. By the end of the film, Moose Jaw exists only fictionally as a parodic site for the inscription of Hancox's lost childhood memories, for his obsessive search for some centre, some ground that never existed anyway. A decentered film, then, by a displaced experimental film-maker, about a simulated prairie city in a radically disjointed Canadian culture. The particular brilliance of Moose Jaw is that there are finally no beginnings or endings, no sure meanings, just random bursts of energy and delocalized memory traces. The mood of the film is about melancholy, sadness, and pathos to such a point of mania that it becomes parodic. In the end, who is really under surveillance? Who is the detached, alienated observer? Hancox or all those abandoned traces of buildings in Moose Jaw? Who is boosting whom? The "Moose Boosters" as cheerleaders for the flagging spirits of the people of Moose Jaw, or all those wonderful dinosaur machines, with their glittering teeth and dull roars, serving one last function to boost the drooping egos of the Moose Boosters?

And finally, is Moose Jaw a brilliant contribution to the tradition of Canadian experimental-film, or something else? The body and mind of Rick Hancox, the film-maker, is itself possessed by the enigma of Moose Jaw to such a degree of intensity that Hancox himself becomes the real subject of this film, an experimental site for playing out the existential drama of the Canadian absurd? Think about it: on the westward train, Hancox may read about crash theory, but on the way home, on the train down east, his splayed face made grotesque against the train window, the surrealistic camera movements, the flashlight searching in the dark for all of the kitschy signs of history, make of him the first of all the crash cinematographers. Hancox, then, as that rarity of film-makers: an artist who sees so deeply that his filmic craft actually does a big flip, making of his body a certain sign that there is a little bit of Moose Jaw in the very best of us.

The Last and Best of all the Postliberals

The writings of Jean-François Lyotard are like Hancox's Moose Jaw. If his meditations can be so deeply melancholic and tinged with nostalgia for a past that does not yet exist, it is because he is a crash theorist. His writings evoke culture in ruins. Not simply the postmodern absurd or the death of a small prairie city caught up in the technological maelstrom, but the death of western metaphysics under the impact of a technologically constituted virtual reality; and not only the death of a "metaphysics of unity," but its melancholic slide into the listless rhetoric of language games. Indeed, Lyotard makes of himself a witness to technological violence. All of his writings are in the way of an intensely personal search for a new mediation point, a regulatory principle between the relativism of a "politics of opinion" and an ethical ground for political judgement. Just like Hancox, Lyotard is driven by the primal of ethics, and by the compelling artistic struggle for thinking the *aesthetic* grounds of capitalist society through to its moment of highest acceleration and possible distortion. A dualistic thinker, Lyotard is haunted by the traditional liberal problem of seeking a satisfactory synthetic principle for fractured experience: opinion versus rational terrorism, desire against inertia. But unlike Hancox, he has not yet passed beyond theory to the slime slide of the film-maker. He has not yet splayed his face against the window of culture, making of himself an experimental X-ray of events which were previously thought to be on the outside. Lyotard stands outside, and still remains independent of his object of study.

And why not? If his writings can be so popular in the United States, it is because he is the last and best of all the American pragmatists. Not really in the tradition of James, Dewey, and Pierce but in the more contemporary tradition of Rorty. A pragmatist of "language games" who seeks to do nothing less than rewrite Kant's *Critique of Political Judgement* in the postmodern idiom: to construct, that is, the grounds for a prudential theory of political justice which would simultaneously absorb and withstand the "incommensurables" and "incongruities" of competing political discourses. That Lyotard is ultimately inconsistent in his quest for a pragmatic ethics is no dishonour since he is, after all, the theorist of paradox, ambivalence and "strange projections." Indeed, the pleasure of "thinking Lyotard" is to be in the presence of an always "doubling discourse:" a phenomenologist in his refusal of the "*grand récits*" of modernism, yet a Marxist in his polemical defence of the Algerian popular revolution against French colonialism; a sophist in his insistence on constructing a "rhetoric of political justice," yet a Nietzschean in his understanding of the artist, Duchamp, as the model for cultural inquiry in the third millennium; a transformation point for recuperating suppressed "minor languages" in contemporary politics, yet a nostalgic pragmatist who falls back repeatedly into the hegemonic language of all text, no sex, which typifies works ranging from *Just Gaming* and *The*

Postmodern Condition to *The Différend*.² This is one thinker who can write an aesthetic theory of *Driftworks* as a direct autobiographical expression of his own philosophical drifting: across the entire spectrum of phenomenology, Marxism, Freudian psychoanalysis, Duchampian aesthetics, deconstructionism, and pragmatic language theory.³ All this is entirely brilliant because at the centre of each of Lyotard's philosophical excurses is a daring artistic maneuver: a ceaseless quest for the "hinge," the "turning," the "transformation matrix" that would make possible a "politics of incommensurables."⁴ Lyotard is the pioneer of postliberal ideology in the age of virtual reality.

To meditate on Lyotard, then, is to enter a big crash scene after the catastrophe where we live at the end of rational politics, economy, and culture. A twilight time where the "rational terrorism" of western metaphysics may stand unmasked, but we live ambivalently, uncertain of the language by which we may articulate a politics and an ethics in the absence of the grand recits of reason. Not a serene time, but an age of fantastic social turbulence and upheaval in which the residues of rational terrorism continue to maintain their stagnating hold on the human imagination, but challenged all the while by the insistent pressure of voices from the underground: the "minority" voices of the suppressed and excluded which seek to trace their signature across the "graphy" of the social text. A paradoxical time in which reality simply vanishes, becoming the nowhere space of technological virtuality, and yet historically specific and politically incommensurable discourses continue to be spoken. Consequently, Lyotard presents us with the paradox of a postliberal subjectivity that is lived at the edge of a "Moose Booster" (for a "pragmatics of obligation") and the tragic sensibility of a memoried artist.⁵

Fading Subjectivity

Lyotard's intellectual biography rubs against the great referents of western civilization. A self-professed sophist in the classical tradition of Antiphonius, the first fifteen years of his intellectual life were committed to a full-fledged Marxist politics in the historical context of the Algerian revolt against French colonialism.⁶ A phenomenologist in the tradition of Merleau-Ponty, all of his intellectual life has been devoted to a suppression of *actual* life experience in favour of an increasingly aestheticized theory of politics and society.[7] A thinker who seeks to operate under the pragmatic injunction of "following nature," his perspective collapses into increasingly frantic searches for identity, from a failed phenomenology and a failed Marxism, to an ultimately grid-locked theory of political judgement and aesthetics.

Lyotard likes to discuss his work in terms of its "eclecticism" and "abstraction." However, in this he is profoundly mistaken. His thought bears no trace whatsoever of eclecticism, but is a systematic working-out of the sophist's imagination: from a tragic theory of culture and society to its attempt to ground a theory of ethics on something other than a "politics of opinion," and to make of incommensurable genres of discourse (the *différend*), the basis for the recovery of a "minority language." This is a language of the social pluralities that have been suppressed in the West by the commodity terrorism of capitalist hegemony and in the East by the "rational terrorism" of bureaucratic Communism.[8] And far from being "abstract," Lyotard's thought is historically specific to the extreme: from the writing of *Economie libidinale* as a decisive rupture with orthodox Marxism to his brilliant artistic studies of Duchamp as a way of theorizing the aesthetic grounds of contemporary liberal subjectivity.[9]

Lyotard also likes to talk fondly about "no identities, only transforma-tions."[10] Just perfect, because that is his own intellectual personality: a mind operating as a nowhere zone which, lacking any internal principle of identity, defines itself in relationship to the great polarities of experience. Thus, for example in *Discours/figure* the self is a dynamic mediation between its entrapment in the language of abstract significa-tion and its displacement in the games of aesthetic figuration.[11] In *La Phénoménologie*, the self is a tragic living mediation of a process of human experience, which is fractured between existence and meaning. In *The Différend*, the self is a tensile point between its immersion in a mere "politics of opinion" and the possibility for a new ethics of political judgement. In *Duchamp*, the self is a "hinge," which in its most creative moments, seeks to act as a transformer, fusing the ascetic labor of technological society with a critical aesthetics of perspective.

Well beyond his own particular life circumstance, Lyotard's intellectual biography has a larger historical importance. Like a space-shifter from science fiction, Lyotard is the first of all the virtual selves: a possessed individual who is possessed by the seduction of virtual reality, and who continuously recreates his identity in relationship to the passage of his subjectivity through the principal axes of technological experience. There are, therefore, always two Lyotards at work in each of his texts. The "visible" Lyotard who makes of his identity the mythology within which it is involved, sometimes a pleasure-seeking Freudian, at other points a static phenomenologist, or a latter-day Marxist living as a civil servant in Algeria, and more currently a pragmatist much in the tradition of Richard Rorty reducing ethics and politics to the rhetorical rules of a language game.[12] There is also a second shadowy Lyotard, the "invisible" Lyotard, the signature of whom is traced in negative form across the pages of each of his writings. In his fifteen years as the Algerian correspondent for the famous French (post-orthodox) Marxist collective, *Socialisme ou Barbarie*, it is the invisible, but tangible, presence of a Marxist theorist who, like a priest who has lost the faith, still dispenses a rhetoric of salvation to others, which he himself not only believes illusional, but an instance of dogmatic hegemony. In his first recreation as a phenomenologist in the tradition of Merleau-Ponty, the invisible Lyotard is the thinker who loses himself in the static dualisms of the phemenological imagination as a way of saving himself from committing to Marxism or Augustinian Christianity. In his later appearance as the best of all the pragmatists, there is the hint of another, more "sublime," Lyotard: the earlier unreconciled Lyotard who could write diametrically opposed texts on "indifference" and the need to "intensify affect." And even in his astonishingly eloquent reflections on art, particularly the writings on Duchamp's *Bachelor Machine*, there is the invisible, but very real, trace of a thinker who can think virtual aesthetics so well because his thought is, first and foremost, deeply materialistic. Here, finally is a French thinker who rubs his knowledge of Algerian labor history—the production of laboring bodies hardened to a point of violent intensity by the machinery of colonializing capitalism within which they operated—across the visible text of Duchamp's aesthetic optic.

Thus, two Lyotard's: the visible, always transformative thinker, the French dilettante, whose subjectivity actually fades away as it passes through the simulacra of pragmatism; and the hidden sublime Lyotard, the theorist who only reaches a tentative destination to be already on his way to another meeting point, always under the sign of "follow nature."

This is to say that Lyotard is, for all his protestations, decidedly *not* a Kantian philosopher, but a brilliant example of Kant in ruins, of the disappearance of Kant's *Critique of Judgement* into virtual subjectivity. A schizoid subjectivity which, functioning in the classical liberal language of the search for a new regulatory principle, has actually already become something quite novel: a "human transformer" which absorbs the raw data of experience as a way of mutating it, a frantic processing of the visible as a way of appeasing, for a moment, the bad infinity of the search for the "unrepresentable." In a curious case of philosophy assuming the living form of biology, Lyotard is the first of all the "viral Kantians": a thinker who makes of his body a sacrificial site for the violent doubling of the visible and the invisible, the presentable and the unrepresentable. Which is why, perhaps, if Lyotard can write so eloquently about the recuperation of "minor languages," of the founding of a theory of political judgement in the incommensurablity of discourses, it is because he is really discussing the means by which he can finally connect the fading grounds of his own subjectivity with his external political circumstances. If Lyotard can comment so often on the "tragic" sense of politics, the "death of history," the "death of culture," and the "death of society," it is because there is no tragic sense at all in his search for the recovery of the suppressed sense of his own sublime. This is one "regulatory principle" that always needs to kick-start itself, to re-energize its fading energies, by sucking in the language of its opposite sign-form. Consequently, Lyotard is engaged in the search for libidinal intensities as a counter-point to the objectivism of dialectical materialism, the appeal for a plurality of minor languages as a way of re-energizing the otherwise pragmatic universe of *Just Gaming*, the ceaseless appeal for a theory of political judgement as a means of re-enchanting an intellectual life that has been stripped of its earlier political commitments. Like a NASA spacecraft on its way to Neptune and Jupiter in the outer galaxy, Lyotard's thought follows a predictable and highly systematic trajectory in which it accelerates by passing through the gravitational fields of different planets, and slingshots past them on its way to another destination.

This is not to say that Lyotard is a philosophical poseur, at least in the traditional sense. His is the postmodern mind, the mind which operates as a big transformer machine. That is why of all his extensive writings, the most critical are his writings on art. Here, in occluded form we find the internal semiurgical grammar of contemporary politics. And why not? Lyotard is transparent about the importance of art. It is a model of how power functions in culture and society. Study Lyotard's Duchamp, then, as a physicist of postmodern politics.

The Sophist's Manifesto

Lyotard has only a *possible* subjectivity, but it enables him to enter the artistic imagination of Duchamp with brilliant eloquence. Lyotard's text, *Duchamp's Trans/formers*, is a book that, abandoning with finality the repressive bar of representation, relaxes its aesthetic optic to that point where Duchamp's *unpresentable*—his playful implosion of the rational terrorism of the law of Euclidean perspective—finally etches its way onto the surface of visibility. Like in Duchamp's *Glass* where two mirrors held at right angles capture in the infinity of their impossible optical regression a foreshadowing of our own refraction into the dissimulative space of virtual reality, so too Lyotard's *Duchamp's Trans/formers* is a theoretical *Glass*. A rhetoric of art, which if it still reads as an internally coherent meditation on four of Duchamp's key works, it is only to camouflage the mutation of Lyotard's writing into a kind of *Bachelor Machine*: a machinery of dissimulation and assimilation which retains the geometrical and perspectival space of language only to reconfirm its disappearance into a world that is virtual to the extent that it no longer possesses a "real" referent. To read Lyotard's Duchamp is finally to enter into the aesthetic non-space of post-Euclidean geometry, and yes of post-Euclidean politics and society.

Which is only to note that if Marx and Engels could write the *Communist Manifesto* as a triumphant proclamation of the objectivistic laws of dialectical materialism and of the emancipatory potential of the proletariat as the historical agent of class struggle, then Lyotard could write his book on Duchamp as a *Sophist's Manifesto*: a celebration of the end(s) of dialectics, reason, class, the perspectival illusions of all the "*grand récits.*" Make no mistake. This is not a text about art, but about proto-art; not about Duchamp, but about *our disappearance* into the "mechanical asceticism" of the age of fetishized technology; not about reason, but about the vanishing of reason into artistic imagination; and not even about the "nostalgia for simulation" but about the multiple, incongruent and fully incommensurable spaces of a "hinged" universe, a universe that is all a matter of "projections," "vanishing gateways," and "partition-walls."[13] Not sophistry as simply a philosophical perspective recovering the more classical empirical impulse to construct morality on the grounds of an errant naturalism, but a hyper-sophistry for the age of "virtual nature." Here, Lyotard provides a political translation of Aristotle's admonition that to "every discourse there must be another opposing it in a rigorously parallel manner, but leading to opposite conclusions." Suddenly, as if we have phase-shifted through the gateway of Duchamp into an alternate reality, we are suddenly in the midst of a greater game.

Lyotard is blunt: it is a conflict between artists and reasoners, the *Bachelor Machine* versus industrial mechanics, sophistry versus philosophy, dissimilators versus assimilators, paradox versus conviction, mirroring versus the specular, "hinged" reality versus the dogmatic optics of Euclidean geometry, the possible versus the present. This is not art criticism at all, but a prolegomenon to a new critique of political judgement. And why not? Following in the tradition of Nietzsche, de Chirico, and Max Ernst—all of whom realized that in the purely perspectival simulacra of cynical power that aesthetics is an experimental testing-ground for new patterns of political thought—Lyotard reads Duchamp as a metaphor of political rule. No longer art versus reality now, but art as *the performative-principle* of the virtual universe; and not aesthetic theory in contradistinction to political theory, but aesthetic theory as the most advanced expression possible of new patterns of emancipatory political thought. Duchamp, then, as the preeminent political theorist of the third millennium. Or, as Lyotard says:

> But the discovery of incongruences and incommensurabilities, if one brings it back from the space of the geometrist to that of the citizen, obliges us to reconsider the most unconscious axioms of political thought and practice. If the citizens are not discernable, if they are, for instance, both symmetrical in relation to a point (the center, which is the law) nonetheless non-superimposable on one another...then your representation of political space is very embarrassed. And if you haven't despaired of your life on the pretext that all justice was lost when incommensurability was lost, if you haven't gone running to hide your ignoble distress beneath the nobility of a great signifier capable of restoring this geometry, if on the contrary you think, like Yours Truly, that it's the right moment to render this geometry totally invalid, to hasten its decay and to invent a topolitical justice, well then,

you've already understood what a Philistine could be doing searching
among the little notes and improvisations of Duchamp: materials,
tools, and weapons for a politics of incommensurables.[14]

Lyotard is correct. Sophistry *is* the basic philosophical structure of
virtual reality. Consequently, if he can comment on Duchamp with such
cool aesthetic precision, if he can reverse and intensify Duchamp's
insights on perspective with such devastating significance, it is because
Lyotard's *Duchamp Trans/former* is in the way of a fateful homecoming.
Maybe Duchamp's world was always on the receding horizon of
Lyotard's intellectual journey. Maybe the act of travelling into Duchamp's
world of "impossible superimpositions, strange projections, special
turning points, anamorphoses, incongruences," represents a profound
achievement of what Lyotard always aspired to in his other intellectual
journeys, from phenomenology through Marxism, but could never
attain: "virtual freedom." A strange new world where subjectivity is lived
as a relative "projection" at the hinge of deeply incommensurable realities,
where personality has no meaning outside of the fully relational world
of politics and society, and where individuality operates in the language
of paradox, irony and ambivalence.

That is what Lyotard really teaches us: we live in the age of sophistry.
A combinatorial reality marked not only by a "politics of
incommensurables," but also by the cultural creation of a regulatory
principle which, in struggling against hegemony of any particular
discourse, also seeks a theory of justice that would harmonize a world of
necessary incongruences.

That is the real sub-text of Lyotard's Duchamp: an alphabet of virtual
reality. Everything is there. A *virtual labour theory* ("machine asceticism");
a *virtual media analysis* ("any putting into perspective is based on *fait
divers*...mass media is hinged randomly. This order has no reason or
principle, there are only projections...."); a *virtual theory of justice*
("topological justice"); *virtual aesthetics* ["the only possible is a physical
corrosive (like vitriol) that burns away all aesthetics and all callistics. I add:
that burns away all politics..."]; *virtual religion* [Lyotard's invocation of
"paganism" (conventionalism) as a corrosive of the rational terrorism of
the True]; and finally, *virtual selves* (hyper-individualism as a mutating
"transformer machine" that acts as a relay-point for the violent and
explosive movement of energy from site to site).[15]

Therefore, what is this virtual reality but a new cosmology: one that is so compelling because it is based simultaneously on an unrelenting rebellion against "rational terrorism" and a philosophical, then ethical, articulation of the post-technological world of virtuality? Lyotard is persuasive, because he is serious. If he can debunk the great signifiers with such good humour, it is only to make possible a politics of incongruences: a world that we can recognize as a matter of material experience because the hinge-experience only operates to provide us with a different angle of vision on the *same* reality. Lyotard is one thinker who can discuss successively and well the *political hinge* (the incommensurability of the Algerian revolution for French colonialism); the *aesthetic hinge* (the mirroring of *discours* and *figur*), the *language hinge* ("refusing the honour of the name" as the first refusal of minority grammars that will not be silenced); the *psychoanalytical hinge* (Freud's pleasure-principle as the basis of Lyotard's intensification of affect); the *ethical hinge* (the *différend* as a "strange projection" of a possible ethics across an incommensurable universe); and a *bodily hinge* (the new body of post-Euclidean culture as a "partition-wall" against the evisceration of the philospher's mirror). Here, everything is a matter of double discourses, of the asymmetry of the "*dissoi logos*" of the early Sophists. Not dialectics, but the four-dimensional space of virtuality; not localized subjectivity, but mutating transformations; not the epochal polarities of the myth of modernism, but pure energetics. Virtual reality is a world that can be so riven by materialism because it is the domain of *Les Immatériaux*, the name that Lyotard once assigned to an immensely creative exposition on virtual reality which he curated at the Pompidou Center in Paris.

Indeed, Lyotard's seduction derives from the fact that his is a proletarian theory of the age of crash technology. There is no nostalgia here for the separation of technology and ethics, no prescriptive remedies for politics and culture outside the transformer machine of virtual technology, but only a therapeutic attitude of critical realism. Lyotard's world *actually* begins with the construction of subjectivity by the norms of technology, and if his vision of political ethics ultimately does not represent a going beyond the horizon of the technological dynamo, if it appears sometimes to acquiesce in the fetishization of technology, it does not diminish its lasting importance as an almost medical diagnosis of the human condition under the sign of liquid technology. So, for example, Lyotard's labour theory, "machine asceticism," sinks its roots directly into popular consciousness when he speaks eloquently of the construction of a new labouring body attuned to the velocity and violence of machine aesthetics.

> The hardness of which we speak is this: Pushed, seduced into factories, into mines, the ex-peasants are placed before an unacceptable challenge, for instance, to work with a 20,000-Hz noise in their ears. They accept it. How? By transforming their bodies; for example, the noise gets neutralized in the auditory spectrum. The metamorphosis of bodies and minds happens in excitement, violence, a kind of madness (I have called it hysteria, among other things). It includes outrageousness, immoderation, excessiveness, when there is no common measure between what you're coming from (the old body) and where you're going. Always incommensurability, here in the projection of the human figure, starting from a familiar space, on to another space, an unknown one.[16]

In a style remarkably similar to John Berger's (the novelist) romantic description of the labouring bodies of the French peasant class as they moved from feudalism to industrial mechanics, Lyotard brings to life the reciprocal challenge of proletarian labour. Not labour as *jouissance* ("The French think it means the euphoria that follows a meal washed down with Beaujolais"), and not labour as repressive prostitution, but something very different. As Lyotard states:

> You miss the essential...the energy that spread through the arts and sciences, the jubilation and pain of discovering that you can hold out (live, work, think, be affected) in a place where it has been judged senseless to do so. Indifferent to sense, hardness. Something that Machiavelli reserved for the Prince, *virtu*.[17]

And so, the old body of the "European aristocrat/peasant" cracks apart and the beginning of something novel emerges: a *virtual body* that, while created in relationship to the disciplinary strategies of the machine, struggled to recover its subjectivity, its own incommensurability, by speeding up the machine to the point of violent implosion. A crash body for a crash technology: now that's Machiavellian 'virtu' for the age of virtual reality!

And not just labour as hardness, as an unceasing demand for the "hinge" of incongruence between subjectivity and machine, but a whole "senibility of *virtu*": from paganism as the religious vocation of crash bodies and philistinism as its public rhetoric, to sophistry as the politics of paradox. In this world, the old European body is shed, and a new pan-European body fit for the age of technological liberalism takes its place. In that age aesthetics can "burn away" all repression-hypotheses because as the first of all the organic transformer-machines this new body is fully enucleated within the horizon of the technological dynamo. Having no horizon of otherness, it learns to speak from within the enfolded technological region of incommensurables, incongruences, and ambivalences. What is this then, but the body as a tensile "partition-wall:" a hinge between the minor language of the possible and the majoritarian grammar of the present. Consequently, Lyotard's aesthetics are an early warning system of the big shift of the cultural residues of the old European body into the common market body: the *hardened* body of the virtual world of technological liberalism.

Consequently, Lyotard's *Duchamp Trans/formers* has a specific ideological importance. Like the energetic and purely processual world of transformers that it describes, it charts out in advance the future of European politics. Everything is there. The mutation of the European body into a transformer-machine, the reduction of ethics to a relational "language game," the valorization of a politics of judgement (how else to distinguish between ontologically equal incommensurables?), a panic search for identity which, like the laws of mechanical thermodynamics, alternates between the inertia of indifference and the ecstasy of intense affects, the flipping of the mass media into a theatre of hyper-reality, the recovering of a pagan sensibility as a way of burning away the nostalgia for the terrorist signifiers. Lyotard's text is not an apathetic apology for the European way, but a doubled discourse. An unconscious meditation on the European mind which, recognizing its entrapment in the dynamic language of technology, seeks to make of its conceptual prison-house an alternating zone of bliss and despair.

Cynical Sentimentality

The early Christians read Virgil, the theorist of the Roman Republic, with the same deadly fascination as we now read Lyotard because they recognized in him a thinker with something to say. Lyotard is the European Virgil, a thinker who can attract such real fascination because he writes in advance the philosophical charter of the United States of Europe—pragmatic ethics.

Indeed, if there can be such a deep affinity between Lyotard's proclamations in defense of pragmatism and the American mind, it is because his blend of ethics and pragmatism recommends itself to an American cultural landscape in which ethics has been burned away by the corrosive of instrumental activism. An improved American, and thus fit to be the first of all the new Europeans in the age of technological liberalism, Lyotard's pragmatism is the necessary illusion that makes palatable the preservation of the pragmatic spirit as the essence of the postmodern way. Not an appeal for the abandonment of the Euro-American "way," for a final flight into indifference (the sin of *acedia*) nor for the celebration of frenzy (which would only be "intense affectivity" unleavened by inertia), but something much more daring, yet comfortable. Lyotard is the theorist par excellence of cynical sentimentality: the pragmatic spirit which is finally rendered coeval with freedom, a civilizing moment. In his thought, there is no requirement to abandon faith in naturalism as the emblematic sign of pragmatism, only to discover its "virtual doubles"—incommensurables, incongruences—as the impossible refractions that confirm the pragmatic ethos as a necessary condition of (our) preservation. Nostalgic, yet projective; deconstructive, yet synthetic; sophistic rhetorical games, yet of immanent ethical conviction; tragic, yet hip: this is the contemporary (Lyotardian) translation of the classical practice of the *dissoi logos*, the practice of doubling discourses.

Consequently, if Lyotard can be so esteemed, not only in his native France but throughout the English-speaking intellectual community, it is probably because he has accomplished the impossible. He is the creator, then apologist, for a *doubled pragmatism*: a theory of politics, culture, and society so faithful to the ancient sophistic advice of "follow nature" that it makes of the traditional fault-line of sophistry its major strength. Not deterred by the mutability of nature, by the tendency for the randomness of events to upset the most elaborately constructed syntheses of pragmatic ethics, Lyotard absorbs randomness, mutability, incommensurablity, and incongruity as the organic language for a new pragmatism. This latest version of the pragmatic way markets itself as a deconstructive "language game," which is its own, probably necessary, intellectual subterfuge. After all, there can be no language game in

Lyotard's writings for the simple reason that there is no language (that too has disappeared into the virtual world of the *dissoi logos* where language reappears in the majoritarian expression of cybernetics and the minor voices of embodied poetry), and no games either (only transformer machines). Lyotard's genius lies in his writing the aesthetic strategy of Duchamp across the political text of the Euro-American way. The strange projections of the *Bachelor Machine* become the inner semiurgy for doubling pragmatism. And all this in the spirit of civil humanism.

After Lyotard's meditation on Duchamp, everything is in the way of a brilliant after-burn: a relentless, but increasingly dispirited, questioning of what shall we do now in a hinged reality, a split reality, in which the dense weight of the present grates against the possible lightness of the future? Indeed, Lyotard is an outstanding practioner of split consciousness—the emblematic psychological sign of the postliberal mind in its full pragmatic expression. He is a Kantian to uphold the possibility of grounding justice in a theory of politics, yet a sophist to deny the possibility of extracting reason from the rites of political history. A Kantian apologist (Lyotard always avers to Kant's "regulatory Idea," the *horizon* of a future possible as a ground for political justice), yet a sophist rhetorician when it is necessary to denounce the "rational terrorism" of Marxism. He discloses a perfect schizoid consciousness in which the struggle for a "politics of incommensurables" necessitates a last desperate search for a new regulatory principle: in epistemology (*La Condition postmoderne* is all about the split in contemporary knowledge between scientific-technical knowledge and paradoxical consciousness); in ethics [*Just Gaming* privileges Kant's 'Idea' as a regulative principle mediating the politics of opinion (perfectly relativistic) and an (immanent) politics of justice]; in history (*The Différend* reduces history to a "language game" divided between prescriptive and skeptical narratives); in aesthetics (*Driftworks* traces the signature of a virtual world cleaved between abstract (hegemonic) aesthetic signification and libidinal art); and, finally, in autobiography (*Peregrinations: Law, Form, Event* revives the Kantian sublime ("the clouds of knowing") as a means of reconciling aesthetics, politics and history.[18]

If Lyotard can be so insistent of discovering a new regulatory Idea, maybe it is because all along he has not been writing a critique of political judgement but a theory confirming the impossibility of a liberal theory of political judgement, ethics and of liberal aesthetics. Perhaps Lyotard's thought is not a celebration of incommensurability, heterogeneity, and difference, but a disclosure of a politics of transparency: a world in which difference and heterogeneity *must appear* as a way of recharging the flagging energies of the postmodern condition. Maybe the desperate search for a new regulatory principle, the *différend* with its litigious rules for settling political differences, is simply the transformation of "conditions of preservation" into absolute predicates of existence. In this case, Lyotard would be the philosopher of cynical judgement. Not of a social universe divided into the incommensurables of opinion and ethics, but of these two polarities as refracted signs in the same system of symbolic exchange. A virtual world that can be intensely cynical because things are in reality perfectly transparent, congruent, and commensurable. Lyotard, then, is not the convenor of an new synthesis of ethics and power, but the author of a fantastic elaboration of the structure of cynical judgement. A world filled with the clouds of illusion—the trompe l'oeil, of heterogeneity, difference, and incommensurability—as ways of masking the mutation of the will to power into the "will to judgement." A will to judgement which seeks to save the appearance of things at all costs by imposing on experience an always artificial (virtual?) unity. Consequently, a frenzied theatrical presentation of a new morality play, the *différend*, is rehearsed as a means of suppressing knowledge of the disappearance of all the "grand recits" into cynical signs. The violent reality, therefore, of a crash society—what Lyotard describes as the "death of politics," the "death of ethics"—is overcoded by a nostalgic philosophical rhetoric for the return of the ethical legislator, the Kantian judge in the kingdom of "transcendental apperception."

We have been this way before. Think of Camus's meditation on the entwinement of judgement and murder, or of Nietzsche's reflections on the "last man" in the cold days of a dying rationalism. Yet, perhaps this is not Lyotard's project. Maybe his is not the "waiting philosophy" of the passive nihilists, but the more actively instrumental perspective of the suicidal nihilists: those who, Nietzsche warned, recognizing that there is no longer any substantive purpose to their willing, would always prefer to go on willing anyway. "They would always prefer to will, rather than not will at all."[19] These are the sacral devotees of the will to will: the will to power, the will to truth, the will to judgement. Yet, whereas Nietzsche studied the will to power only to announce its dissolution into cynical power, and unlike Foucault who meditated deeply on the will to truth only to observe chillingly its disappearance into a "language without roots...a sex without a ground,"[20] Lyotard is different. He has explored the will to judgment, not to understand the nihilism within, but in the more insipid hope of translating the will to judgement, the play of heterogentity and difference, into a dispensation for an emancipatory political history. His is the philosophical optic on the ruling illusions necessary for the preservation of the age of technological liberalism.

Consequently, the lasting importance of Lyotard may be more histori-cal than philosophical. His might be the story of the inversion of the Freudian obsession with the pleasure-principle into the ideology of the hysterical male. In his philosophy, the male dream for the abstract social unity of the transcendental signifier finds its moment of fateful culmina-tion: a theory of justice that can only speak of regulating "our prescriptives"; a materialist theory of the social as a "suprasensible nature"; a reflection on language which strips words of aesthetic memory, political power, and historical specificity; a theory of the body that still holds to the desexualized notion of "phenomenological totalities." The male dream is a hystericized philosophy laced with great equivocations: pagan, yet all the while extolling "Kant's Idea of the totality of reasonable beings"; triumphantly skeptical, yet (ethically) dogmatic; rhetorical (the art of the sophists), yet philosophical (the "reasoners"); driftworks, yet libidinal intensities; a brilliant interpretation of art (Duchamp), yet an exhausted philosophical reprise of the "pragmatics of obligation." A perfect model for the pragmatic dream, which is to say for the hysterical male dream, of *weak theory*: a doubling philosophy which, just as Nietzsche said in *The Genealogy of Morals*, allows them to set down their chairs in the middle..."That is what their smirking tells us."

7

Cynical Aesthetics:
The Games of Foucault

Three Games

Even as I meditate on the postmodern body as both the object and privileged after-image of a colonizing power, the words begin to fade into a laconic and fatal disintegration. I remember, I *must* remember, the bitter words spoken by Michel Foucault in the first volume of *The History of Sexuality* that "(P)ower as a pure limit set on freedom is, at least in our society, the general form of its acceptability":[1] the limit, that is, which makes bearable our instatiation within a cynical and indifferent freedom.

Yet perhaps it is no longer, as Foucault theorized, the radical play of domination and freedom with the *self* as a contested space of absence (the famous recovery of an "unspoken subjectivity"), but domination under the sign of cynical power as a *mise-en-scène* of the truth of the postmodern body as a Bataillean site of recklessness, discharge, and upheaval. When we have already passed beyond the first two orders of sexuality, beyond organic sex and discursive sexuality, to the third stage of a hyper-real sex (where the body is doubled in an endless labyrinth of media images, where transgression is the law, and bodies alternate between hermeticism and schizophrenia), then even Foucault's privileging of the second order of discursive sexuality (where we must pass through what is *said* about our sexuality, its *discourse*, in order to finally know the truth of our sex) now works only to suffocate the grisly implications of a hyper-real, cynical sex.

As such, Foucault's fate was to be the last and best of all the Cartesians: the theorist who on the clinical grounds of medicine, power, sexuality, and science thought through the bitter analytics of the "thinking subject," of ratiocination to excess, even as rationality secreted into the very constitution of the ethical subject, and emerged finally as the enucleating horizon of western experience. If Foucault could never think beyond the dark side of Kant, could never escape—whether in his interpretation of science as cynical truth, medicine as cynical power, or panoptic space as the cynical gaze—the trap Kant had laid for him (just as Nietzsche could never break beyond a modernist entanglement with the question of the death of God); if Foucault could never free himself from a resolutely modernist entanglement with Kant's nominalism on the question of the death of truth; and if Foucault could not finally avoid the complicity of his own theory with the unfolding disaster of the "games of truth"; this is not to deny that there is everything to be gained and everything at stake, in meditating anew on the games of Foucault. For they are simultaneously the limit and possibility of his theoretical legacy.

First, Foucault was a theorist of political transgression par excellence whose meditations on "relational power" could evoke such an impassioned mood of political resistance (the emancipation of subjugated knowledge) because all his reflections of power were leavened with the hard knowledge that transgression, far from representing an experience of rupture, now works only to confirm the impossiblity of traversing the *limit experience*.

Second, he was a historian of the quantum kind—ironic, ambivalent and paradoxical on the question of the irreality of the historical moment—

who could simultaneously refuse historical totalizations in the form of the will to power and nothing else, and then work to create a double recuperative moment: the famous method of historical genealogy with its privileging of zones of knowledge with low epistemological profiles; and a marked preference for plural histories of local subjectivity, a hyper-materiality of pleasures and desires, not value. Ultimately, Foucault was of the peculiar order of reluctant historians: one who who refused history as a game of truth, only to install in its place the game of *effective history*, a "history which descends."

And third, Foucault was an anti-epistemologist who could be so relentless in tracking down the discursive networking of the "games of truth"—in sexuality, science, penology, and psychiatry—since all along he was the latest of the philosophical exponents of the logic of quantum science, of a quantum epistemology which functions by mirroring *code elements* (the constitutive conditions of possibility of a structural sex, a structural power, and a structural madness) *and local historical practices*. Probably against his own theoretical intentions, Foucault's thought was the breaking-edge of the advanced liberal mind with its full aestheticization of knowledge. His discourse was also that of the dying days of the liberal *episteme* with its relational power, relational truth, and regulatory ethics finally achieving self-reflection. A murderer of the old humanist author, Foucault was also an inscribed "local subject" who fulfilled Unamuno's precept: "I am I in the human circumstance and the human circumstance is I."

Foucault's thought, then, was the fully modern liberal mind at the height of its times. In him alone you see them all, because this was the aestheticized liberal mind at its most intense and acute point of auto-critique, brilliance, and ambiguity: simultaneously a master parody of the fate of the panoptic body and an ironic meditation on the fate of a relational, sidereal, and topographical postmodern scene. Consequently, in Foucault alone there are to be found all of the key panic sites at the fin de millennium.

Panic Science: This is Foucault's early encounter with Canguilhem where science is forced to confess its secret: that it was never anything more than an irreal cosmology, and one in which, moreover, the object of scientific investigation was, in the deployed form of power/knowledge, a prime after-image and constitutive condition of justification for the scientific *episteme* itself.

Panic Medicine: Foucault's genealogy of the discourse of the clinic reveals the great epistemic shifts in medical discourse for what they always were: the inscription of a shifting social physics and its associated hieratics of the body and exclusionary power strategies onto the purely fictional and topological terrain of what French intellectuals these days like to call—*Quel Corps?*

Panic Madness: Not just the suppression of the imagination into silence by the will to truth of psychiatry; not just, that is, Blake's dark dream of the sleep of reason begetting the monsters of *Madness and Civilization,* but all panic suppressions:

— the *panic power* of *Discipline and Punish* where the prisoner entombed within the gaze of the panoptic is reduced to a silhouette, and in which the jailer is also entangled in a deep complicity with the eye of power, of which he is a necessary rhetorical function.

— the *panic gender* of Herculine Barbin, the real story of whom is not so much about the normalization of sexuality under the patriarchal, religious, and psychiatric gaze (as Foucault will claim), but about a gender and a body which is not allowed to be spoken—the *woman's body* of Herculine Barbin, and about the dream of another sex which must be suicided because it is insurrectionary.

Panic Erotics: Foucault's last two books—*The Care of the Self* and *The Uses of Pleasure* focus on the reduction of the body, in Athens and Rome, to an "aesthetics of existence," to a tutelary regime of the moral problematization of pleasure. These texts can be disappointing to some because they recover (brilliantly) the erotic subject only to reveal this erotic subject as a panic site. For Foucault's erotic subject is colonized from within by the publicization of dream life in Artemidorus, where dreams are empty sign-systems waiting to be inscribed by all the primitive myths: inscribed, that is, from without by an *aphrodisia*—an "aesthetics of experience"—which are regulatory not only of the care of the *bodily humors,* of pleasure under the sign of high aesthetics, but also of marital relations and the erotic *recits* of "boys loving boys." *The Care of Self* and *The Uses of Pleasure* are texts about panic erotics: that moment when the body disappears into an empty sign, interpellated by all the ideologies, tattooed by the pleasures of a fully aestheticized sexuality, and inscribed by the languages of medicine, philosophy, and *oneiroheureutics.*

Waiting for Augustine

In short, *Panic Foucault* is at hand, a thinker whose particular brilliance is that he actually became what he sought to describe: a *sliding signifier*, oscillating between the suffocating antinomies of modernist discourse, between a grisly and clinical examination of the production of cynical power, cynical truth, cynical sex, and cynical language; and a famous, but ultimately futile, attempt to recover the *truth of sexuality* in a meditation on Athens, Rome, and Jerusalem. Like Freud's Michelangelo before him, Foucault awoke to find himself in the midst of the nightmare he thought he was only dreaming. He was a thinker with no exit, because in his meditations of the truth of sexuality (an aesthetics of pleasure), Foucault could never think through the truth of the Christianity of Augustine. Like the Roman stoics before him, and that peculiar strain of Greek skepticism before them, Foucault ended his life with the melancholy resignation of intellectual futility; that is, the consciousness of entrapment within the nightmare of the infolded technologies of self to which he had awoken. He ended up where he began: in psychiatry, in the torture chamber of the tattooed self.

Fourth-century Christianity was not a continuation of the Greek and Roman theories of the self, nor their simple and abrupt reversal, but, at least in the writings of Augustine, a *solution* to a fundamental crisis of the self, which neither the Greeks with their "aesthetics of existence" nor the Romans with their reduction of the self to a purely juridical and corporative concept rooted in *dominium propertium* could resolve.

What Foucault in his last writings avoids, and as a fallen-away Cartesian *must avoid*, is that neither rationalized ethics nor materialistic conceptions of bodily pleasures could provide a directly experienced mediation of the antinomies of existence.

Consequently, when calamities arose, whether in the form of the Athenian plague of the fifth-century B.C. or the failure of the Democritean ideal of democracy or the bitter sense of fatalism and intellectual futility that swept the Roman imperium when, at the height of its power, the corrosive question arose—now that we have conquered an empire, now that we have become the sign itself of empire for whom the spear is our symbol, a restless will to survive at any cost our dominant psychology, and the acquisitive spirit of private possession our most cherished belief—

what are to be the ultimate ends of empire?[2] How, that is, and *why* go on willing when there are no longer substantive purposes to the ends we choose, in a universe indifferent to the choices we *will* in full freedom?

While the Greeks and the Romans moved ultimately in the grip of fatal necessity, the Christians, and Augustine specifically, solved the crisis by making the self an *individual psychology*; and, moreover, produced a vision of the self, not just the confessing self but also the ecstatic self, as a directly experienced mediation for summoning into a new *episteme* all the divided antinomies of the classical experience of Athens and Rome. Against Athens and Rome with their purely *external principles* of unity—the moral problematization of the pleasures into an aesthetics of experience on the one hand, and the reduction of the self to an instrument of private property on the other—the early Christian thinkers held out the possibility of a hyper-materialist theory, not only of bodily pleasure, but also of bodily suffering. In their eschatology, the principle of unity of western experience was finally rendered internal to the psychology of self. Indeed, in the Augustinian vision, metaphysics *secretes* into the bodily tissues, making the body a *will* and nothing besides. It was from Jerusalem, not Athens or Rome, that the self as a constitutively nihilistic will to power began to spread out. Foucault's "confessional self" as an early warning system of panopticism misses the whole point of the Christian negation that subordinated the body—will, intelligence, and feelings—to the exterminist sign of the Trinity. Ultimately, the directly experienced Trinitarian body—the western body — with its breaking of the will into itself, with its new starting-point in individual psychology, is the real truth of Christianity, of which Foucault's theses on the confessing self and the panoptic are sociological diversions, reflecting as they do only the reified manifestations of the already exterminated body.

Foucault missed the secret truth of Christianity by reading the Christian body under the sign of the panoptic, "confessing self," and was condemned to recapitulate in his own life and death the fatal necessity, the tragic sense of futility, and the last dark laughter of the parodist, of Greek enlightenment. If *The Care of the Self* could end bleakly by noting the sterility of the philosopher's virtue for "boys loving boys,"[3] this was because Foucault's mind was, once again, an outbreak of the (classical) dialectic of enlightenment. In his thought, the melancholy play of chance that ultimately dashed the best intellectual hopes of the Athenians and made intellectually futile the miltant and imperial ambitions of the Roman stoics is recapitulated with such intensity that Foucault must have known that he was only awaiting another Augustine.

The game of Foucault was a daring and brilliant one. As a philosopher whose thought transgressed the white space of indifference, Foucault always said that his intention was

> to examine both the difference that keeps us at a remove from a way of thinking in which we recognize the origin of our own, and the proximity that remains in spite of that difference which we never cease to explore.[4]

This is the game of the intellectual imagination, of life and death, to such a point of melancholic excess and brilliant intensity that thought begins to fold in on itself, making Foucault a marker of the postmodern fate.

His is the self-confession of the fully exhausted late modernist mind, the mind of the dying days of aestheticized liberalism, which functions only to confirm the impossibility of the mythic legacy of the dialectic of enlightenment. If, for example, Foucault could end his life with two texts on the constitution of the sexual self as an ethical subject and an analytics of sexual austerity, it is because, in these last works, Foucault finally came home to his Kantian self. Permitting himself the discontinuity he had always permitted others, Foucault's meditation returned to the project that runs through all his theorizations on medicine, science, power, and psychiatry: that is, studying intently the "conditions of possibility" for our enucleation within the will to truth, the will to sexuality, and the will to power as our own *primal*.

Having reflected on cynical power and cynical truth too deeply ever to be content with the phenomenological reductions of Merleau-Ponty and too much a tragician on the matter of the discursive infolding of power ever to make his peace with Sartre's moralizing historicism, Foucault, finally, was that rarity: an unfinished, radically discontinuous, and ambiguous thinker.

The lasting fascination and seduction of Foucault's games is less philosophical or political than, perhaps, purely literary. It may someday be written that reading Foucault is perceiving how the liberal mind at the fin de millennium liked to think of its history (genealogical, but with possibilities for rupture), its epistemology (nominalist, but later nomist), its ethics (a little cynicism, a little piety), its theory of politics (the Kantian regulatories), its power (relational and topological), and its theory of the self (trapped in a continuing debate among Athens, Rome and Jerusalem).

Foucault's legacy would then be that he is the latest of the elegant tombstones of the dying days of aestheticized liberalism. If he could be so deeply evocative, it is because his entire theorization with its brilliant meditations on the cynical analytics of power, sexuality, truth, and madness is also a clonal after-image of an age that has already ceased to exist.

Epilogue

TERMINAL CULTURE

As one whose identity is deeply entwined with the unfolding of the technological dynamo in the North American context, what is compelling about contemporary French thought is its searing meditation on terminal culture as well as its profound *political* reflection on the ruling rhetoric of technology in the empire of speed and power: the American hologram. Here, finally, is a theoretical vocabulary and a language of decolonization for piercing the closed horizon of technology, and for listening intently to the "intimations of deprival" in the midst of the celebratory ruins of the American way. For a North American, then, the specific appeal of the French discourse on technology is a deeply ethical one. The French mind discloses both a brilliant theoretical diagnosis of the breakthroughs and breakdowns of the virtual world, and a resistance strategy for living in a culture tattooed by digital reality. Not an ethics of political resistance formulated outside the dominant assumptions of technology and power, but one that is constituted *within* the algorithmic codes of the virtual world. To reflect upon the French, is to finally understand America flipped inside out, with its ideological software (the rhetoric of technology) on the outside and its dynamic hardware (the *actual* forces of technology) on the inside. Read Baudrillard as a clinical diagnosis of the disappearance of America into digital reality; Barthes as a theorist of the empire of the (American) sign; Deleuze and Guattari as a description of the rhizomatic flows and decodings involved in becoming-America; Foucault as a historian of the genealogy of (liberal) nihilism that finds its *apogée* in American bourgeois subjectivity; and Lyotard as the most eloquent of all the American pragmatists. No longer, therefore, French theory as a mirror of technology, but a reflection from beyond its dynamic horizon of the *virus* of technology in the empire of the American postmodern.

Indeed, if contemporary French thought divides into two warring camps—melancholy skepticism and pragmatic naturalism—that is because power can only be understood in a schizoid way as a doubling of subjectivity and signification. Not, therefore, the old *dualism* of American thought and practice, but a relationship of *imminent reversibility* between primitivism and hyper-technology as the DNA of the American hologram. Virtual America as the materialization in real historical practice of that which could only be *thought* by the French: an empire of the cynical sign.

From its beginnings, America has always been the world's first purely poststructuralist society. Consequently, what exists only *theoretically* in the French mind is experienced *practically* in the flipping of American power (and personality) between radical skepticism (leavened by the pragmatics of cynicism) and viral positivity (horizoned by the fading dream of technology as freedom). In this case, the French discourse on technology is the memoried residue, long after the fact, of the meeting of the primitivist will to mastery of social and non-social nature and the instrumentalities of technique in the ground of the virtual world that is American eschatology. The French mind is a theoretical autobiography, all the more brilliant for its intellectual exhaustion, of the rhetoric of the American (technical) way.

Photograph: Linda Dawn Hammond
Charlie (Three Part BodySeries)

Notes

1

1. Albert Camus, *The Fall*, New York: Vintage, 1956, pp.117-118.

2. Camus, *The Rebel*, New York: Vintage, 1956, p.291.

3. Ibid., p. 299.

4. Ibid., p. 300.

5. Jean-Paul Sartre, *The Critique of Dialectical Reason*, trans. A. Sheridan-Smith, London: Verso, 1982.

6. Michel Foucault, *History of Sexuality: Vol. I*, trans. R. Hurley, New York: Pantheon Books, 1978, p.86.

7. Jean-Paul Sartre, "Czechoslovakia: The Socialism that Came in from the Cold," *Between Existentialism and Marxism*, trans. J. Mathews, New York: Pantheon Books, 1974, p.100.

8. Peter Sloterdijk, *Critique de la raison cynique*, trad. H. Hildenbrand, France: Christian Bourgeois, 1987; see particularly "Cynisme — Crépuscule de la fausse conscience," pp. 25-32.

9. Jean-François Lyotard, *The Différend: Phrases in Dispute*, trans. G. Van Den Abbeele, Minneapolis: University of Minnesota Press, 1988.

10. Paul Virilio, *Esthétique de la disparition*, Paris: Galilee, 1980.

11. Michael Weinstein, "Thinking the Death Camps with Heidegger," unpublished manuscript.

2

1. Virilio, *L'Horizon négatif*, Paris: Editions Galilée, 1984, pp. 143-164.

2. For an excellent discussion on the aesthetics of the war machine, see Virilio, *War and Cinema: The Logistics of Perception*, trans. P. Camiller, New York: Verso, 1989.

3. Virilio, *Pure War*, trans. M. Polizotti, New York: Semiotext(e), 1983, p. 89.

4. Virilio, *Speed and Politics*, trans. M. Polizotti New York: Semiotext(e), 1986, p. 47.

5. Tony Brown, *Day Dreams*, Winnipeg Art Gallery, Sept.- Oct. 1986.

6. Virilio, *Pure War*, p. 39.

7. The threefold method of "tactics, strategy and logistics" that Virilio develops in *Pure War* is concretely exemplified in the epistemological studies of *War and Cinema*.

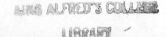

8. "Speed as destiny" is the central thematic of a number of Virilio's texts, ranging from *L'Horizon négatif* and *L'Inertie polaire*, to *Esthétique de la disparition*, to *Pure War* and *Speed and Politics*.

9. See particularly, Virilio, "La dromoscopie," *L'Horizon négatif*, pp. 143-164.

10. Virilio, *Speed and Politics*, p. 141.

11. Ibid., p. 30.

12. Ibid., p. 46.

13. Ibid., p. 47.

14. This theme links *War and Cinema* and *Pure War*.

15. Virilio, *Speed and Politics*, p. 64.

16. Ibid., p. 135.

17. Fredrich Nietzsche, *On The Genealogy of Morals*, trans. W.Kaufmann and R.J. Hollindale, New York: Vintage, 1967, p. 163.

18. See especially, Virilio "Esthétique de la disparition," *L'Horizon négatif*, pp. 99-117.

19. Virilio, *Speed and Politics*, p. 77.

20. Ibid.

21. Nietzsche, *Genealogy of Morals*, p. 127.

22. Chris Dercon, "An Interview with Paul Virilio," *Impulse* 12(4) (Summer 1986): pp. 35-38.

23. Virilio, *L'Horizon négatif*, p. 28.

24. Virilio, *War and Cinema*, p. 6.

25. Ibid., p. 7.

26. Ibid., p. 51.

27. See especially, Virilio's description of technologies of "derealization." Ibid., pp. 79-89.

28. The body without will—a "metabolic vehicle"—finds its cinematic parallel in the appropriation of the human retina by the sign machine in *War and Cinema*.

29. Virilio, *War and Cinema*, p. 33.

30. Ibid., p. 85.

31. Jean Baudrillard, *La Guerre du Golfe n'a pas eu lieu*, Paris: Editions Galilée, 1991, p. 49.

32. For Virilio's most elaborate theory of "disappearance," see: Virilio, *Esthétique de la disparition*, Paris: Galilée, 1980.

33. George Grant, *Lament for a Nation*, Toronto: McClelland & Stewart, 1965; *Technology and Empire: Perspectives on North America*, Toronto: House of Anansi, 1969; *Philosophy in the Mass Age*, Vancouver: Copp Clark, 1959; *Time as History*, Toronto: Canadian Broadcasting Corporation, 1969.

34. Grant, *English-Speaking Justice*, Sackville, New Brunswick: Mount Allison University, 1974, p. 83.

35. Ibid., pp. 84-85.

36. Ibid., p. 93.

37. Virilio, *Pure War*, p. 28.

38. Ibid., pp. 38-39.

39. Ibid., p. 50.

40. Grant, *Time as History*, Toronto: Canadian Broadcasting Corporation, 1969, p. 52.

41. Virilio, *Pure War*, p. 18.

3

1. Friedrich Nietzsche, *On the Genealogy of Morals*, trans. Walter J. Kaufmann and R.J. Hollingdale, New York: Vintage, 1969, p. 85.

2. See particularly, Jean Baudrillard's "Magic and Labor," in *The Mirror of Production*, trans. M. Poster, St. Louis: Telos Press, 1975, pp. 81-84.

3. Baudrillard, *The Mirror of Production*, p. 113.

4. Baudrillard, *La Transparence du mal*, Paris: Editions Galilée, 1990, p. 78. "L'homogénéisation des circuits, l'univers idéal de la synthèse et de la prothèse, l'univers positif, consensuel, synchrone et performant constituent un monde inacceptable."

5. Baudrillard, *For a Critique of the Political Economy of the Sign*, trans. C. Levin, St. Louis: Telos Press, 1981, pp. 143-163.

6. Baudrillard, *The Mirror of Production*, p. 114.

7. Ibid., pp. 114-115.

8. Which is only to say that Baudrillard's texts, from *L'Échange symbolique et la mort* to *Seduction*, are scenes of sacrificial violence: a challenge to the "rationalist eschatology."

9. Baudrillard, *The Mirror of Production*, p. 143.

10. Ibid., pp. 142-144

11. Ibid., p. 113.

12. All of Baudrillard's texts, ranging from *Simulations* to *The Ecstasy of Communication*, read social space against the grain of quantum physics.

13. Marshall McLuhan, *Counter Blast*, Toronto: McClelland & Stewart, 1969, p. 42.

14. Nietzsche, *Genealogy of Morals*, pp. 125-134.

15. Madonna interviewed by Forrest Sawyer on ABC's *Nightline*, December 3, 1990.

16. Baudrillard, *La Transparence du mal*, foreward, p. ix.

17. This would make, therefore, Baudrillard's *Seduction* the dark twin star of Sartre's *Critique of Dialectical Reason*.

18. Jean Baudrillard, *L'Échange symbolique et la mort*, Paris: Gallimard, 1976, pp. 15-73.

19. Jean Baudrillard, *The Ecstasy of Communication*, trans. B. and C. Schutze, New York: Semiotext(e), 1988, pp. 13-14.

20. Ibid., p. 27.

21. Marshall McLuhan, *Understanding Media: The Extensions of Man*, Toronto: McGraw-Hill, 1964, p. 64.

22. Marshall McLuhan, "Joyce, Aquinas, and the Poetic Process," *Renascence* 4(1) Autumn 1951: pp. 3-4.

23. The cold obscenity of communication is the theme that haunts all of Baudrillard's work, from *Simulations* and *The Ecstasy of Communication*, to *Cool Memories*.

24. "The world exists..it lives on itself: its excrements are its food." Friedrich Nietzsche, *The Will to Power*, trans. W. Kaufmann and R.J. Hollindale, New York Vintage, 1967. See also Arthur Kroker, "Cynical Power," in Kroker and David Cook, *The Postmodern Scene*, Montreal: New World Perspectives, 1986, pp. 114-131.

25. Baudrillard, *In the Shadow of the Silent Majorities*, trans. P. Foss et al, New York: Semiotext(e), 1983, p.69.

26. Baudrillard, *Simulations*, trans. P. Foss et al, New York: Semiotext(e), 1983, p. 55.

27. Baudrillard, *Silent Majorities*, p. 68-69.

28. Baudrillard, *Forget Foucault*, New York: Semiotext(e), 1987, p. 46.

29. For Baudrillard's most eloquent description of the "resurrection effect," see his discussion of cynical power in *Forget Foucault*, p. 61.

30. Baudrillard, *Seduction*, trans. B. Singer, Montreal: New World Perspectives, 1990, p. 61.

31. Ibid., p. 62.

32. Ibid., pp. 64-66.

33. Ibid., pp. 63-64.

34. Ibid., see particularly the essay, "*Trompe l'oeil* or Enchanted Simulation," pp. 60-66.

35. Baudrillard, *Forget Foucault*, p. 45.

36. Baudrillard, *Seduction*, pp. 63-64.

37. Jean Baudrillard, "L'objet et son destin," *Les stratégies fatales*, Paris: Bernard Grasset, 1983, pp. 161-255.

4

1. See especially, Roland Barthes, "The Metaphor of the Eye," *Critical Essays*, trans. R. Howard, Evanston, Illinois, Northwestern University Press, 1972, pp. 239- 247.

2. Roland Barthes, *The Pleasure of the Text*, trans. R. Miller, New York: Hill and Wang, 1975, p.40.

3. Ibid., p.64

4. Ibid., pp. 38-39. "No significance (no bliss) can occur, I am convinced, in a mass culture (to be distinguished, like fire from water, from the culture of the masses), for the model of this culture is petit bourgeois."

5. Ibid., p. 44.

6. Ibid., pp. 57-58.

7. Barthes, "The Last Happy Writer," *Critical Essays*, pp. 83-89.

8. Ibid., p. 89.

9. "We modern men are the heirs of the conscience- vivisection and self-torture of millennia: this is what we have practiced longest, it is our distinctive art perhaps, and in any case our subtlety in which we have acquired a refined taste." Nietzsche, *Genealogy of Morals*, trans. W. Kaufmann and R.J. Hollindale, New York: Vintage, 1967, p. 95.

10. Barthes, "*Will* Burns Us...," *Critical Essays*, p. 7.

11. Barthes, *The Pleasure of the Text*, pp. 40-42.

12. Barthes, *The Fashion System*, trans. M. Ward and R. Howard, Berkeley: University of California Press, 1990. Barthes's description of fashion as a "rhetorical system," is a brilliant reprise on the pleasure of the consumer, on a nihilism which is "in some ways interior to institutions." See particularly, the conflation of rhetoric and fashion as a poetics of clothing, pp. 225-273.

13. Barthes, *The Rustle of Language*, trans. R. Howard, Berkeley: University of California Press, 1989, p. 77.

14. David Easton, *The Political System: An Inquiry into the State of Political Science*, New York: Knopf, 1971.

15. Talcott Parsons, *The Social System*, Glencoe Illinois: Free Press, 1951.

16. Barthes, "The Imagination of the Sign," *Critical Essays*, pp. 210-211.

17. Barthes, *The Fashion System*, p. 27.

18. Ibid.

19. For a discussion of the rhetoric of the "image-repertoire," see Roland Barthes, *Image/Music/Text*, trans. S. Heath, Great Britain: Fontana/Collins, 1977.

20. Barthes, *The Pleasure of the Text*, p. 40.

21. Ibid., p. 43.

22. Ibid., p. 42.

23. Ibid., pp. 38-39.

24. Jean Baudrillard, *In the Shadow of the Silent Majorities*, New York: Semiotext(e), 1983, p. 1.

25. Barthes, *The Pleasure of the Text*, p. 64.

26. Barthes, *Mythologies*, trans. A. Lavers, New York: Hill and Wang, 1972, p. 155.

27. "This is the case with mythology: it is a part of both semiology inasmuch as it is a formal science, and of ideology inasmuch as it is an historical science: it studies ideas-in-form." Barthes, *Mythologies*, p. 112.

28. See especially, Barthes's "The Jet Man," which is one of the best existent descriptions of the mutation of hardware and software into a new form of hybrid intelligence—"wetware." *Mythologies*, pp. 71-73.

29. Barthes, *The Eiffel Tower and other Mythologies*, trans. R. Howard, New York: Hill and Wang, 1979,

30. Barthes, *Mythologies*, p. 142.

31. Ibid., p. 138.

32. Ibid., p. 145.

33. "Myth Today," Ibid., pp. 109-159.

34. For Barthes's political postulates on the ideological basis of myth, see *Mythologies*, pp. 148-155.

35. Ibid., p. 155.

36. Ibid.

37. Barthes, *Empire of Signs*, trans. R. Howard, New York: Hill and Wang, 1982, and *Image/Music/Text*.

38. Barthes, *Camera Lucida: Reflections on Photography*, trans. R. Howard, New York: Hill and Wang, 1981, and "Plastic," in *Mythologies*, pp. 97-99.

39. Barthes, "The Structuralist Activity," *Critical Essays*, p. 219.

40. Ibid.

41. Ibid., p. 215.

42. Ibid., p. 220.

43. Octavio Paz, "The Prisoner," *Early Poems: 1935-1955*, Bloomington Indiana: Indiana University Press, 1973, pp.89-93.

5

1. Gilles Deleuze and Félix Guattari, *Anti-Oedipus: Capitalism and Schizophrenia*, trans. R. Hurley et al., New York: The Viking Press, 1972, p. ii.

2. Ibid., "A Recapitulation of the Three Syntheses," pp. 106-113.

3. "Significance is never without a white wall upon which it inscribes its signs and redundancies. Subjectification is never without a black hole in which it lodges its consciousness, passion, and redundancies." Gilles Deleuze and Félix Guattari, *A Thousand Plateaus: Capitalism and Schizophrenia*, trans. B. Massumi, Minneapolis: University of Minnesota Press, 1987, p. 167.

4. Deleuze and Guattari, *A Thousand Plateaus*, pp. 174-177.

5. Ibid., pp. 167-191.

6. Deleuze and Guattari, *Anti-Oedipus*, pp. 9-16.

7. Deleuze and Guattari, *A Thousand Plateaus*, "Year Zero: Faciality," pp. 167-174.

8. Deleuze and Guattari, *Anti-Oedipus*, pp. 68-113.

9. See especially, Gilles Deleuze, *Kant's Critical Philosophy*, trans. H. Tomlinson and B. Habberjam, Minneapolis: University of Minnesota Press, 1984.

10. Deleuze and Guattari, *Anti-Oedipus*, "Capitalist Representation," pp. 240-262.

11. Ibid., "Preface," by Michel Foucault, pp. xi-xiv.

12. Ibid., pp. 190-191.

13. Deleuze and Guattari, *A Thousand Plateaus*, "1730: Becoming-Intense, Becoming-Animal, Becoming-Imperceptible..." pp. 232-309.

14. "This is because the two groups are like determinism and freedom in Kant's philosophy: they indeed have the same "object"—and social production is never anything other than desiring-production, and vice-versa—but they don't share the same law or the same regime." Deleuze and Guattari, *Anti-Oedipus*, p. 378.

15. "In reality, everything coexists..." Ibid., p. 377.

16. Deleuze and Guattari, *A Thousand Plateaus*, p. 262.

17. Ibid., pp. 262-263.

18. Benedict de Spinoza, "On the Improvement of the Understanding," *Spinoza Selections*, ed. J. Wild, New York: Charles Scribner's Sons, 1930, pp. 1-44.

19. Deleuze and Guattari, *A Thousand Plateaus*, p. 254.

20. Ibid., pp. 256-257.

21. Ibid., pp. 260-265.

22. See especially, "1933: Micropolitics and Segmentarity," pp. 208-231; "1837: Of the Refain," pp. 310-350; and "Smooth and the Striated," pp. 474-500 in ibid.

23. Gilles Deleuze, *Coldness and Cruelty*, New York: Zone Books,1989.

24. Deleuze and Guattari, *On the Line*, New York: Semiotext(e), 1983.

25. As the philosophical horizon of the twentieth century, Nietzsche's "truth is dead" ultimately issues in Baudrillard's "dead power," Foucault's "cynical ethics," and Sloterdijk's "cynical reason."

26. Nietzsche, *Genealogy of Morals*, trans. W. Kaufmann and R.J. Hollindale, New York: Vintage, 1969, p. 454.

27. Georges Bataille, "The Use Value of D.A.F. de Sade," *Visions of Excess*, trans. A. Stoekl, Minneapolis: University of Minnesota Press, 1985, pp. 94-95.

6

1. *Richard Hancox*, Toronto: Art Gallery of Ontario, 1990.

2. Jean-François Lyotard, *Just Gaming*, trans. W. Godzich, Minneapolis: University of Minnesota Press, 1985; *La Condition postmoderne*, Paris: Les Editions de minuit, 1979; *The Différend: Phrases in Dispute*, trans. G. Van Den Abbeele, Minneapolis: University of Minnesota Press, 1988.

3. Lyotard, *Driftworks*, ed. R. McKeon, New York: Semiotext(e), 1984.

4. See especially Jean-François Lyotard, *Duchamp's Trans/Formers*, trans. I. McLeod, Venice, CA: The Lapis Press, 1990.

5. Lyotard, *Just Gaming*, pp. 93-95.

6. Lyotard, "La Guerre 'contre révolutionnaire,' le société coloniale et le Gaullisme," *Socialisme ou barbarie*, 5 (25) (juillet- aout 1958): pp. 20-27.

7. Lyotard, *La Phénoménologie*, Paris: Presses Universitaires de France, 1954.

8. Lyotard, *Just Gaming*, pp. 94-95.

9. Lyotard, *Economie libidinale*, Paris: Les Editions de Minuit, 1974.

10. While most explicitly discussed in Lyotard's *Duchamp's Trans/Formers*, the "parti-pris" of "no identities, only transformations" is the hinge which doubles all of his writings, from *Driftworks* and *Discours, figure*, to *Just Gaming* and *Economie libidinale*.

11. Lyotard, *Discours, figure*, Paris: Klincksieck, 1971.

12. See especially, Richard Rorty, "La cosmopolitisme sans émancipation: en réponse à Jean-François Lyotard," *Critique*, 41 (456) (mai 1985): pp. 569-580; and "Discussion entre Jean-François Lyotard et Richard Rorty," ibid., p. 584.

13. Lyotard, "Hinges," *Duchamp's Trans/Formers*, pp. 117-199.

14. Ibid., pp. 27-28.

15. Lyotard's *Duchamp's Trans/Formers*, is that point where virtuality bursts beyond the domain of art, becoming the genetic code—the digital DNA—of social experience.

16. Lyotard, *Duchamp's Trans/Formers*, pp. 18-19.

17. Ibid., p. 16.

18. Lyotard, *Peregrinations: Law, Form, Event*, New York: Columbia University Press, 1988.

19. Nietzsche, *Genealogy of Morals*, p. 163.

20. Michel Foucault, *The History of Sexuality: Volume I*, trans. R. Hurley, New York: Pantheon, 1978, pp. 93-98.

7

1. Michel Foucault, *The History of Sexuality: Volume I*, trans. R. Hurley, New York: Pantheon, 1978, p. 86

2. Charles Norris Cochrane, *Christianity and Classical Culture*, Oxford: Oxford University Press, 1980, chapters 2 and 3.

3. Foucault, *The Care of the Self: Vol. 3*, New York: Pantheon, 1986, Part 6, "Boys," pp. 187-232.

4. Foucault, *The Uses of Pleasure: Vol. 2*, New York: Vintage, 1986, p.7.

Printed in Canada